CHURCH HURT, WOUNDED & LEFT FOR DEAD

"HOW TO OVERCOME"

JOSHUA VALLAIRE

DEDICATION

I would like to first give all honor and glory to the Father, the Almighty God of Abraham, Isaac, and Jacob. To my Lord and Savior, Yeshua HaMashiach, also known as Christ the Messiah, and Jesus the Christ. I also thank the Holy Spirit, the Comforter, who enables me to live a righteous and faithful life and teaches me the ways of the Kingdom of God.

This book is dedicated to my late mother, **Ella Mae Rankins**, and to my living father, **Joshua Jay Vallaire Sr.** I also dedicate this to my oldest sister, **Endia Vallaire**, and her family, my youngest sister, **Shareca Vallaire**, and her family, and my brother and friend, **Lavoy Vallaire**, and his family. I love my family dearly.

I am also inspired by and love my children, **Telvyn, Terry, Joshlyn, and Terryll Vallaire**, and their families. I give thanks to all the pastors and leaders who have nourished me throughout my life. I have had the privilege to walk with them and witness both the blessings and the challenges of leadership, guiding people from all walks of life, nationalities, cultures, and beliefs.

A special thanks goes to my friends and colleagues, **Minister Janet Hasty, Kizzy Henderson Dr. Rose Cooks, Pastor Karen Washington, Pastor Beverly Leday**, for walking with me during some of the darkest days of my life. Their faith and constant encouragement to trust God through His Word helped sustain me through difficult times. I also extend my gratitude to all the family and friends God placed in my life, teaching me valuable lessons along the way—you know who you are.

I also want to honor my late grandmother, **Fannie Williams**, for her unwavering support, along with my grandfather, **Bishop Alfred Williams Sr.** I am deeply grateful to my late uncle and godfather, **Kenny Carrier**, who provided me with shelter and advice during challenging times, and to my godmother, **Apostle Marie Carrier**, for her prayers and leadership. My cousins **Venus, Chassity, Mackenzie**, and their children also have my gratitude for their love and support through all seasons of my life.

Lastly, I would like to express love and appreciation to my **Uncle June Alfred Williams Jr.** and his family, **Apostle Paul Allen Williams** and his family, **Anthony Williams** and his family, **Alice Williams** and her family, **Jeannie Richardson** and her family, and **Vivian Rankins** and her family. Thank you for being part of my journey.

TABLE OF CONTENTS

INTRODUCTION

Joshua Vallaire Jr. is a man of many talents and an unwavering commitment to serving others. With over 25 years of experience in electrical engineering, he has contributed his skills to some of the most esteemed companies in the industry, including Texas Eastern Pipeline, Duke Energy, Solar Turbines, and GE Power. As a Senior Electrical Engineer at General Electric Power for a decade, Joshua was instrumental in developing innovative products and embracing cutting-edge technologies. His leadership, communication, and business management skills were sharpened during this time, allowing him to provide invaluable mentorship and entrepreneur training to others.

Currently, Joshua continues his career in engineering at ReCon Engineering Management Services, but his influence extends far beyond his professional roles. As the CEO and founder of **Come Home Shelter**, Joshua leads efforts to combat homelessness by partnering with community leaders and nonprofit organizations to make a lasting impact. His passion for helping others is further demonstrated in his work with **Vallaire Management Services, LLC**, where he manages musical artists and supports young entrepreneurs in achieving their business goals.

Joshua's commitment to service is rooted in his deep faith. Raised in ministry, he is an active member of **Eternity Full Gospel Fellowship** and collaborates with **Glory Believer's Center, Alter of Fire, Faith Family Church** to build up men's ministries. His spiritual journey is grounded in a dedicated prayer life, including fasting and prayer, and he actively operates within the fivefold ministry, embracing all gifts of the Spirit.

Beyond his spiritual and engineering work, Joshua has founded **Vallaire Enterprises, INC**, a company dedicated to empowering communities and individuals through support, development, and Kingdom building. Whether it's providing resources for minorities, aiding the impoverished, or promoting business strategies for established enterprises, Joshua's vision is to manifest the will of God on earth by creating lasting change in the lives of people.

From his roles as an engineer to a community leader, mentor, and spiritual guide, Joshua's multifaceted journey is a testament to his relentless dedication to making a difference in the lives of others. This book delves into his incredible journey, highlighting his achievements, challenges, and the unwavering faith that drives him forward.

CHAPTER 1

MY TRANSFORMATION PROCESS FROM NO LIGHT TO LIGHT

INTRODUCTION

A journey from darkness to light is an odyssey that relates to the soul and is much more about the most integral part of our being. This is such a journey for me, personally, because it is one that started from a space of emptiness and hopelessness, a period in my life when I was lost without any purpose or aspirations. But it was in this, the darkest hour, that the light of Jesus Christ shone brightest, to turn me toward the path of redemption and renewal.

MY EARLY YEARS

I was raised in a very traditional and cultured family where religion was an active part of my life? Religion seemed to be rule-following instead of being in a relationship with the living God. My childhood was period marked by a search for identity and meaning, but I often found myself surrounded by confusion and turmoil. Upon entering my teenage years, it became quickly evident that the pressures of life and the allure of worldly pleasures would carry me further and further away from any semblance of spirituality, I was trying to fit in.

THE BREAKING POINT

The turning point came in a time of great personal crisis: all sorts of challenges—relationship problems, financial crises, and the general feeling of loneliness—attacked me on evey side. I tried finding comfort in various worldly things, but nothing really helped to fill up the void. It was then, in my desperate moments, that I started questioning the meaning of life and the direction that I was leading.

One night, feeling hopeless and lying in bed, I cried out to a God whom I was not even sure existed. I asked for some type of sign, maybe something that would give me hope or let me know that my life serves a purpose—that I am not alone in this. And it all began that night, my spiritual awakening.

A DIVINE ENCOUNTER

Soon after that desperate prayer, I had an experience that changed my life forever. A friend who had become aware of my distress invited me to a church service. I consented to go, reluctantly, not expecting much. As I entered into the presence of the church, I felt a nice sense of peace. The atmosphere was filled with warmth and love—something I had never felt before.

It was then that, during the service, he lectured about God's unconditional love and Jesus Christ's sacrifice on the cross. His words radiated to the inner core of my darkness-beset heart, and I couldn't help but feel stirred within me. At the end of the service, he welcomed people who wanted to receive Jesus into their hearts to come forward. Without knowing yet quite what it was that I did, I found myself walking up to the front with tears pouring down my face.

Accepting Jesus as Lord and Savior

So, at that moment, I received Jesus as my Lord and Savior. I confessed my sins and let Him take control of my life. Instantly, it was like the biggest weight coming off my shoulders, and the peace and joy that flooded my heart can best be described as profound. I knew right then that I would never be the same again. For the very moment of darkness, which seemed to have overwhelmed me for such a long time, had just been shown the light of God's love.

BEING BORN AGAIN AND BAPTIZED WITH THE HOLY SPIRIT

After coming to know Christ, I was intensely hungry to know more of God. I began to read the Bible voraciously and study it, trying to get a hold on truths which were contained therein. I started attending a local church and fellowshipping with other Christians who encouraged me in my new-found faith.

It wasn't long before I knew that I had to be baptized, publicly declaring my commitment to Christ. The Holy Spirit truly touched me that special day of baptism. Coming up from the water, I knew I had been reborn. I wasn't just born again symbolically but in a real, life-changing way. The Holy Spirit twined his work around my life, in the area or place where he guides, teaches, and empowers me to live a life of faith.

THE ZEAL OF JESUS UPON ME

My new-found faith came with such a zeal to share the love of Jesus with each and everyone around me. I could not just sit with the joy and peace I had, thus I needed to share the good news of change with everybody else. I was involved in numerous ministries in the church and was ready to go out on the mission of serving and starting to effect changes in people's lives for the better.

Joining a New Ministry

As I grew in my faith, I felt a renewed call to come back and now be part of a new ministry of outreach and service to the community. It opened a lot of opportunities to feed the hungry, clothe the poor, and bring hope to the ones who are hurting. So in that context, I really began to grasp what it was to be the hands and feet of Jesus, to love others as He had loved me.

Serving in ministry is very challenging but, at the same time, very rewarding. There are times that it is so tiring to do the work, but as you see the lives of the people being changed because of the love of Christ, you get to feel that it is all worth it. I learned how to be humble, compassionate, and perseverant. And in serving, I've realized and found out that it's not just about my transformation; it's about the transformation of the world surrounding me.

Walking With the Pastor

As I became more involved in the ministry, I found myself walking more closely alongside the pastor. The value of this mentorship instilled in me the guidance, wisdom, and support one obtains for balancing out life in ministry. His example of servant leadership was one of integrity, faithfulness, and a strong dependence on God.

A PASTOR'S ROLE AND RESPONSIBILITIES

Walking with the pastor also gave me insight into the weighty responsibilities of pastoral leadership. I saw, with my own eyes, the sacrifices made, the challenges encountered, and the particular adherence needed to go through with the business of shepherding a congregation. This has greatly heightened my respect for pastors and brought a deeper understanding of the need for leadership support and prayer.

MY DAVID & SAUL EXPERIENCE & CONFLICTS IN MINISTRY

But with the many blessings of ministry, I had huge conflicts and challenges. So, I felt at times when the jealousy and opposition of Saul were coming my way. Misconceptions, hurts, offenses—being rejected became part and parcel of the journey. Yet in the midst, I learned to lean on God's grace and not focus on the attacks against me.

THE OFFENSES CAME

Offenses are a part of any ministry, and I was no exception. Sometimes the hurt from what others did or said went deep. Yet, as time went on, I knew that I was preventing growth and effective ministry. Rather, I had to let those hurts go to God and seek His healing and restoration.

THE REJECTION CAME

Rejection is so painful when practiced within the church setup. There were times when I felt unappreciated and yearned for the recognition of the works I had put into the ministry. Yet again, in prayer and meditation, I found the realization that it's not about men's approval but God's that I should find my worth and validations in.

FALSE HUMILITY, FALSE LOVE

Among these challenges, I also met false humility and false love. Some from the front side use to show humbleness and love for others but their nature and activities were wholly different. I learned from them that discernment is very necessary and to be closer towards the true love and humility shown by our Lord Christ.

FORGIVING THE OFFENDER

One of the most profound lessons I learned was on forgiveness. Bitterness and unforgiveness were weights pulling us back from the fullness of grace. I cannot overstate the importance of forgiveness through prayer, by the power of the Holy Spirit, to release those who wronged me into God's hands.

MOVING ON BY FAITH

The more I walked by faith, the more I saw the faithfulness of God. God was opening new doors and providing for my needs in miraculous ways. Moving on from past hurts and embracing a future with hope, trust in God enabled me to experience His blessings and to grow in my calling.

CONCLUSION

The going from the dark into the light is not ended. Every day is another test of trusting God, walking in His ways. My transformation process proved the power of God's love and grace. While I am growing more in my faith, I have a commitment to sharing the light of Christ with others and to living out His purposes for my life.

PRAYER VERSES ON FAITH

1. **Hebrews 11:1 (NIV)** - "Now faith is confidence in what we hope for and assurance about what we do not see."
2. **Romans 10:17 (NIV)** - " Consequently, faith comes from hearing the message, and the message is heard through the word about Christ. "

PRAYER VERSES ON FORGIVENESS

1. **Ephesians 4:32 (NIV)** - "Be kind and compassionate to one another, forgiving each other, just as in Christ God forgave you."
2. **Matthew 6:14-15 (NIV)** - "For if you forgive other people when they sin against you, your heavenly Father will also forgive you. But if you do not forgive others their sins, your father will not forgive your sins."

PRAYER VERSES ABOUT TRUSTING GOD

1. **Proverbs 3:5-6** - "Trust in the Lord with all your heart, and lean not on your own understanding. In all your ways submit to him, and he will make your paths straight."
2. **Isaiah 26:3-4** - "You will keep in perfect peace those whose minds are steadfast, because they trust in you. Trust in the Lord forever, for the Lord, the Lord himself, is the Rock eternal."

CHAPTER 2

ACCEPTING JESUS AS LORD AND SAVIOR

INTRODUCTION

The day I decided to accept Jesus Christ as my Lord and Savior was the greatest decision I ever made in my life. It marked the beginning of a journey that was deep in transformation, hope, and creating a new sense of direction. This chapter explains those events and experiences that led to such a life-changing decision and how it impacted my heart, mind, and soul.

THE STIRRING OF THE HEART

Before I accepted Christ, life was like a tapestry of confusion and searching for me. I was in disorder and confusion, always seeking for what more could exist in another dimension, and yet hopelessly beyond reach. I had sought and gained some of the successes that this world calls good, but there was an unmistakable emptiness that nothing ever filled. Friends, relationships, material things—in the end, they just gave short-lived fulfillment and left the void in my heart.

It was during this time of personal turmoil that I began to meet people in whose lives I saw peace and a captivating joy. They spoke about a relationship with Jesus Christ—not a religious figure but a personal Savior. Their stories of change and hope did something inside of me. I began to think that maybe there was more to life than what I had been seeing.

THE INVITATION

One day, one of my close friends invited me to their church. Though skeptical, I accepted the invitation out of curiosity about where such unbending faith came from. As I entered into the church, I was greeted with warm reception and real faces that smiled at me. There was such an atmosphere, unlike any other place I had been to—tangible sensations of love and acceptance.

The worship service began, and as the congregation began to sing praises to God, I was overwhelmed by a sense of tranquility. The music, the words, and the people just touched my heart. It felt as though something, like a weight, was slowly being removed from my shoulders. For the first time, hope made its appearance.

THE MESSAGE OF SALVATION

He then began to talk about salvation and how Jesus Christ came to earth to save mankind from sin, and to give them eternal life. The pastor spoke of God's love, so great that He sent His only begotten Son to the cross to die for our sins. As he described the sacrifice of Jesus, I was smacked with a sense of conviction. It was as if he spoke directly to me, speaking into the very emptiness I had been wrestling with.

He said that salvation was a gift, one God was offering free, and that all one had to do was take it by faith. He told us that salvation wasn't about perfection or holding all the right answers but about recognizing our need for a Savior and handing our lives over to Him.

THE ALTAR CALL

At the conclusion of the sermon, he made an altar call for whoever was willing to accept Jesus into their hearts. My heart was pounding in excitement, and I was both afraid and sweetly anxious. I felt this was the moment of decision, a choice that would alter everything in my life. Even as doubts stirred within me, something compelled me to take that step of faith.

I walked forward timidly, my heart shaking in my chest. Standing at the front of the church with others who were making this decision, the pastor led us in a very simple, sincere prayer of repentance and acceptance. I repeated the words, asking Jesus to forgive my sins and come into my life as my Lord and Savior. And then, all of a sudden, that tide of serenity and joy swept over my mind. It could be compared to some light going on in an inner self that evaporated the huge cloud hovering over my heart.

NEW BEGINNING

Accepting Jesus as my Savior was more than a spiritual decision; it was a turning point marking the beginning of a new life. I felt a new sense of purpose and identity. The Bible came alive as one read it, and I began to realize more deeply the love of God for me and the power of His grace. I was no more bound to the mistakes and failures of my past; I was now a new creation in Christ.

The change in me was very apparent to my friends and family. They said I had a different attitude, different behavior, different mood—different everything. The peace and joy I was experiencing did not come on and off, depending on my circumstances; they were in Jesus. I had discovered the answer to that longing in my soul and I wanted to tell this awesome news to everybody I knew.

JOURNEY OF FAITH

This would be a new journey, not easy. At any time when I walked in faith, I grew to face doubt, temptation, and some weak moments. How in the world would I have done that? There were times when I would question my decision and struggle to understand the depths of God's grace. But through it all, God remained faithful, teaching me that I should trust in Him and lean on His strength.

I joined a Bible study group where I could ask questions and learn from others and grow in my knowledge of God's Word. Fellowship and encouragement of fellow believers were priceless, encouraging, praying for me, walking with me through ups and downs throughout this faith journey. I also engaged mentors that would give guidance and wisdom to navigate the complexities of life as a follower of Christ.

BAPTISM (MAKING A PUBLIC DECLARATION)

As I began to mature in my faith, I felt a leading to make another step in my walk: baptism. I wanted everyone to know that I had made a commitment to Jesus and that it was a public declaration showing a transformation occurring in my heart. It was a glorious day. I was baptized in the presence of friends, family, and my community at the church as I went down into the waters, therefore showing the death of my old self. The experience was deep. I felt a deep sense of cleansing and renewal as I came out of the water. It was a physical manifestation of the spiritual reality that already took place in my heart. I knew that I was not making a public statement, but getting deeper refilling in the

Holy Spirit to empower me to live my faith freely and authentically, and rose again, symbolizing the new life which I had found in Christ.

LIVING OUT MY FAITH

After I was baptized, I dedicated my life to living out my faith tangibly. I got involved in the different aspects of church ministry and served excitedly, sharing the love of Christ with others. Whether serving in the community, outreach programs, or just being a friend, I wanted to be a vessel for God's love and grace.

Some of the most rewarding things in this journey were when others came to faith and the actual witness of Jesus' transformative power in their lives. I began to realize that my testimony and experiences could be a means of encouragement and hope to others who were struggling or looking for answers. This realization is what kept me passionate about evangelism and discipleship, as I wanted to help others feel that freedom and joy that I had found in Christ.

CONCLUSION

Accepting Jesus as my Lord and Savior was the most important decision I have ever made. It marked the beginning of a journey characterized by beautiful mountaintop experiences and harsh valleys, yet God's love and faithfulness have never wavered through it all. The change that happened in my life further testifies to the power of the Gospel and the very changing grace of God.

The more I walked by faith, the more I began to see God's goodness, and that lovely gift of salvation, each and every day. I just hope my story can be an inspiration for others to seek out the truth, open their hearts to Jesus, and experience that life-changing power of His love for themselves. You challenge many who have sat on the fence, not knowing what is yet ahead, into that step of faith. Jesus is standing with open arms, ready to take you from darkness into His marvelous light.

CHAPTER 3

BORN AGAIN AND BAPTIZED WITH THE HOLY SPIRIT

INTRODUCTION

There is probably nothing as intense, among the several points of the journey of faith, as being born anew and baptized with the Holy Spirit. This chapter deals with personal testimony on how that powerful encounter with God makes a relationship with a believer better and raises the level of strength for living according to God. This spiritual awakening brought with it greater clarity of purpose and renewed strength to face life's challenges.

THE CONCEPT OF BEING BORN AGAIN

To many people who could not speak Christian, the term probably sounded esoteric or vague. It means spiritual rebirth—a dramatic change of heart and soul—that came through faith in Jesus Christ. The phrase was taken from the conversation which Jesus held with Nicodemus in The Gospel According to John, in which he explained that one should be born of water and the Spirit to see the Kingdom of God.

To me, it was not just intellectual assent to Christian doctrine. It meant the total surrender to the will of God, the recognition of a sinful nature in me, repenting of past wrongdoings, and letting God renew my mind and heart. It meant inviting the Holy Spirit to live in you, directing your thoughts, your deeds, and even your decisions.

After receiving Jesus into my life as my Lord and Savior, I threw myself into the Scripture and prayer. And the more I began to pursue God, the more I would feel something stirring on the inside of me—that behind the scenes of my belief was a growing sense of God's presence and compelling desire to draw closer to Him. This spiritual hunger opened me to teachings about being filled with the Holy Spirit, something I had heard about in church but hadn't fully understood.

One evening, the pastor preached to the prayer service regarding baptism in the Holy Spirit. The feeling behind the explanation was that of being overwhelmed with God, becoming full of His Spirit, with spiritual gifts provided and sensitivity to His presence. When he asked those who wanted this experience to come forward for prayer, I had a great feeling of anticipation and longing. I wanted more of God and to be filled with His Spirit.

BAPTISM OF THE HOLY SPIRIT

After that, I stood wherever I was as I closed my eyes. I prayed from the bottom of my heart, repenting and desiring more from God. The pastor and the prayer team prayed with me, with hands laid on me. From that moment, I began to feel some very strong peace and warmth. It appears like some calm force embraced me.

Next thing, I was overflowing with a deep happiness, and words began to tumble from my lips in a language that I had never known—a spiritual gift called speaking in tongues mentioned in the New Testament. It felt like my spirit was speaking directly to God, beyond the limitations of human language. God's love was so palpable; I went to tears in this very fullness of its intimacy and nearness.

But out of this experience, there was born a new boldness. Here was the milestone in my own spiritual pilgrimage—the baptism with the Holy Spirit. I was given fresh power to experience and live out my religion authentically, dynamically. There was an obvious transformation in my countenance, attitude, carefulness toward the uncovering leading of the Holy Spirit, boldness in witnessing, and a deepening love for God and others.

In the following days, the other spiritual gifts sprung into life: the gift of discernment and prophecy. Though none of these were for my exaltation, they were only to edify the Church or as work of a minister to others. I developed a strong inclination to use the giftings in a way that honored God and provided service to the people of God.

CHALLENGES AND GROWTH

While baptism in the Holy Spirit was in itself a great joy, there were some not-so-easy days to face. There lurked some amount of self-doubt, spiritual battle, and instances of vagueness. I further struggled to understand or operate in the spiritual gifts I received at other times. However, these struggles actually developed into opportunities for growth and deepened dependence on God.

I learned the importance of being faithful in prayer, worship, and reading the Word of God. With the help of mature believers, I could always take every circumstance that comes in the right way. I now know the importance of humility in the knowledge of the gifts and experiences that one does not earn but by the grace of God.

IMPLICATION ON LIFE AND MINISTRY

Being baptized in the Holy Spirit has significantly impacted both my life and ministry. He gave me intimacy or a sense of His presence, where it would make me desire more and more to surrender to His divine will. It opened doors to minister to the church and community in a new way.

I started to orient myself to minister not out of obligation, but because of a true love for God and His people. The concern for the lost people became a part of me, and a desire to see others experience the power of Jesus also came into the system. That might be for me through my preaching, teaching, or just simply being a friend who would attempt to be a channel of God's love and grace.

CONCLUSION

Truly life-changing was being born again and being baptized with the Holy Spirit. That to me was surrendering and allowing God to take control, to fill me with His Spirit. This experience brought new understanding of His love and boldness to share the Gospel, along with increased sensitivity to the leading of the Spirit.

As I tread upon this journey, it reminds me of the need to be filled with the Spirit day by day, to live a life that glorifies God. The journey has not been an easy one, but it is still a fight to keep on. The joy, peace, and purpose in this hesed-derived loneliness and having the Holy Spirit within are unmatched. I pray that others, too, may come into a true, life-altering encounter with God, to encounter and receive the abundant life He has for them.

CHAPTER 4

THE ZEAL OF JESUS UPON ME

INTRODUCTION

Born again, baptized in the Holy Spirit, my life turned radiant and meaningful. The fourth chapter describes the zeal overtaken in me for Jesus Christ and His mission. This was none other than deep passion and did not stand as an emotional high feeling that transformed every bit of life. It fueled my desire to serve, to share the Gospel, and to grow in my faith. This period turned into one of extreme spiritual growth and active ministry.

A NEWFOUND PASSION

This experience in the baptism of the Holy Spirit birthed within me an insatiable hunger for God. I couldn't get enough of reading the Bible, praying, and spending time in worship. It was if a fire had been lit in my soul, and I wanted to know everything about the God who saved me. This passion extended beyond personal devotion; it overflowed into every area of my life, compelling me to share the love and truth of Jesus with all whom I encountered.

It was not without its problems. So many times, I found myself in situations when this new passion clashed with more reserved attitudes around me. Some people labeled my enthusiasm as overzealous or even fanatic. However, I could not help but contain such great joy and urgency. I knew that what I had experienced was real and transformative, and I wanted others to experience it too.

SERVING IN THE CHURCH

My zeal for Jesus naturally led me to become more involved in the church. I searched for every opportunity to serve, whether through volunteering in children's ministry, joining the worship team, or helping with community outreach programs. I felt a deep sense of responsibility to use my gifts and talents for God's glory. Serving wasn't an activity; it was an expression of my love and gratitude toward God.

Some of the most rewarding aspects of this season were definitely the outreach activities in which we participated at church. We organized food drives, visited nursing homes, and even conducted evangelistic events in the community. During each of these encounters, there was an opportunity to share the Gospel of God and to concretize the love of Christ through tangible deeds. I was often amazed by how God used simple acts of service to touch hearts and open up doors for deeper faith conversations.

Evangelism simply became the overflow of my zeal for Jesus. I couldn't keep the Good News to myself; it felt like I was under obligation to share it with whomever would listen: friends, family, coworkers, strangers—anybody and everybody would hear about Jesus and what He had done for me. This was not always easy, particularly with skeptics or hostile people, but the Holy Spirit enabled me to be emboldened and wise.

One of the strongest experiences was serving in a street evangelism team. We used to go around the parks, busy intersections, and other places to share the Gospel with passersby. Intimidating though at first, I quickly realized that people were often more open to hearing about Jesus than what I had anticipated. Many were searching for meaning and hope and welcomed the opportunity to talk about spiritual matters.

These encounters taught me the value of listening and relationship-building. Evangelism was not simply standing before people and preaching; it was being concerned about them and having the will to walk with them in their spiritual journey. I have learned to trust God for results, knowing it is His work through the Holy Spirit to convict and convert, not mine.

CHALLENGES AND GROWTH

The zeal was followed by problems. Not everyone was understanding or appreciative of my newfound passion for Jesus. I began to face criticism, misunderstandings, and even ridicule from people who felt that I had gone overboard. Some accused me of righteousness or judgment, while others simply wrote it off as some sort of phase. These reactions were especially painful when they came from those closest to me.

It was a moment of leaning into God and asking for His guidance. I learned humility and grace—that my role is to love and show truth, not make people believe. And further, I have been taught to identify myself and learn validation in Christ, not in people's approval or acceptance. This was an invaluable lesson for me, in that it helped me to keep faith in and mission steady, irrespective of whatever opposing views were available on the subject.

SPIRITUAL MATURITY GROWTH

I furthered this by growing in spiritual maturity. I surrounded myself with mentors and spiritual leaders who could guide and challenge me. I attended Bible studies, prayer meetings, and conferences, always ready to learn more about God's Word. I also read a lot from famous Christian authors and highly respected theologians, taking up knowledge and perspectives on different aspects of the faith.

One of the most important growth areas was learning discernment of God's voice. There were so many compelling voices and influences that it became infinitely important to be sensitive to the Holy Spirit's leading. This took intentionality in time spent in prayer and Scripture, coupled with wise counseling. The more I grew in discernment, the more confident I was in making decisions and stepping out in faith, knowing God was guiding me.

Another area of growth was balancing zeal with wisdom. Sometimes, I would become so eager to serve or evangelize that my zeal for Christ translated into overexertion in effort or even impulsiveness in action. I had to learn the value of rest, self-care, and establishing healthy boundaries. This reminded me that spiritual growth is a lifelong process; maturity is expressed in patience, perseverance, and a readiness to learn from mistakes.

ZEAL AND ITS IMPACT

The zeal of Jesus changed not only my personal life but also greatly affected all those around me. I witnessed friends and family members give their lives to faith as a result of the transformation they had witnessed in me and the love of Christ shining forth from my life. I saw God move powerfully in the lives of those whom I ministered unto—giving healings, deliverances, and salvation.

This season of zealousness also initiated the foundation for future opportunities for service. I discovered my passion to teach and disciple others, especially people misunderstood and hurting. These experiences shaped my perception of calling and prepared me to take different roles and responsibilities that later came within the church and community.

CONCLUSION

The zeal of Jesus upon me was the most defining period in my spiritual journey. It was a period of passionate pursuit, bold evangelism, and deep growth. Much as it had its share of challenges, it also brought incredible joy and fulfillment. It reminded me that the development of disciples requires all-consuming zeal for following Jesus—surrender, sacrifice, and the willingness to be used by God however He deems fit.

As I reflect on this past season, I am so very grateful for the ways God moved in and through me. The fire that has been lit inside my heart does not stop burning, and I do my best to keep it burning by praying, worshiping, and being obedient to the Word of God. I pray this zeal continues to stay with me and inspires others in growing their relationship with Jesus, living for Him with passion and purpose.

CHAPTER 5

JOINING A NEW MINISTRY

INTRODUCTION

The spiritual journey was an evolutionary process, where the very zeal which drove me into the service and sharing of the Gospel brought about times of conflict and misunderstanding in the old church. Even through the tumult, I feel God directing me to find a new place that would let me keep on growing and serving. This chapter will reflect on joining the new ministry, lessons learned, and how God shaped my faith and calling as I was making this transition.

THE CALL TO MOVE ON

Leaving my former church was not easy. I had come to know quite a number of people, devoted time and even to some ends energy to that place, and I had grown significantly in the Lord there. However, all that had become a very slow process, and it became quite clear that God had directed me elsewhere. With much prayer and the advice from the wisely thinking, I felt such a peace that I knew the right thing to do would be to step away and find a new spiritual home.

It was an exciting, yet daunting call to move on. Exciting for what God had in store for me, yet with the real fear of how I was going to find a new community within which I would feel at home again. I realised that this was to be a challenging journey full of faith, patience, and the ability to step into the embrace of an unknown future, yet reassured that God who was ahead of me—way ahead of me—would make sure that I get just what I need at just the right moment.

A GOOD FIT

Finding a new ministry is a process of prayerful discovery. I visited several churches and ministries. Each had its own culture, style of worship, and approach to ministry. I was looking for a place not only to grow in my spiritual life but also a place I could use the gifts and passions that God has placed within me.

In this process, I learned a lot: it's not about finding a church that you like but finding God's calling for you. I looked for signs of a healthy, thriving community—one emphasizing biblical exposure, authentic worship, and a commitment to serving others. I also made an effort to connect with the leaders and members to hear from them regarding their vision and heart for the ministry.

It was after many months of searching that I finally landed on a church that felt like home. Being a growing church, it had this sense of being big on building discipleship, outreach, and having deep relations between members. From the time that I walked in, I felt the presence of God—not to mention a warmth among the people that did resonate with me. I knew this was where God led me to plant my roots and continue my journey.

ESTABLISHING NEW RELATIONSHIPS

Relationship building was the first thing I did when I wanted to be part of a new ministry. I ensured that I knew people in the ministry, participated in small groups, and took part in church activities. The move helped me acclimatize to the community and establish good relationships with people who shared similar beliefs and values.

Building these relationships was both rewarding and challenging. It was at times difficult for me, because of the vulnerability I had to open up my experience, to trust newer people. But in exchange, it did give support and a sense of belonging. I also realized that the friends I've gotten in the new ministry are not social at all. We are spiritual partners who prayed with each other, encouraged each other, and held each other accountable in our walk with Christ.

These relationships also made room for growth on both ends. By sharing my experiences, I learned from the wisdom and insight of others. This way, through the ideation and support, I grew to maturity in my faith and had so much opened up for me in terms of understanding what it really meant to be part of the body of Christ.

ENTERING INTO SERVICE IN A DIFFERENT WAY

I felt certain ways to get involved as I delved more deeply into that new ministry. My previous experiences put diversified facets of ministry into place, and I was eager to put new settings into practice again with these skills. As I did approach the leadership and indicate all of my interest in contributing, and they welcomed such an interest and were supportive of my involvement.

I started serving in at least a few different capacities and began working with the outreach, discipleship, and worship teams. Each one afforded opportunity to exercise different gifts and develop new ones. New ministry also brought challenges, forcing me to get accustomed to varied styles of leadership, learn new systems, and navigate through different community dynamics. All these challenges were very helpful to the exercise of humility, flexibility, and dependence on God.

Among the most fulfilling aspects of service in this new ministry was seeing God use my past to bless others in the moment. I could use the lessons learned from past challenges and conflicts as tools to help others who might be going through somewhat the same thing. Whether advice, encouragement, or simply a listening ear, I found that God had positioned me well for the moment.

LEARNING TO TRUST GOD IN TRANSITION

Starting a new ministry was such a very critical move in my spiritual journey, and it got to the point of deep trust in God. There were moments of doubt and uncertainty when I questioned whether I had made the right decision. But I kept repeating to myself that God is faithful and that He works everything out for good for those who love Him and are called according to His purpose (Romans 8:28).

This season has brought a teaching for patience, a wait for God's own time. I have learned that transitions are often awkward but make good fertile ground for future great growth. God was really stretching me, pushing past the comfort zones, and teaching me to really learn to depend on Him. In all this, I experienced His provision, guidance, and peace in ways that have served to deepen my faith and trust in Him.

THE FRUIT OF OBEDIENCE

I started seeing the fruit of obedience when I settled into these new ministries. God began to open doors for me to minister among people in ways I had never even imagined. I began to see lives transformed, hearts healed, and people encouraged through this work that God has initiated through my ministry. It's a humbling thing for one to see that the insurmountable God can use one, despite his weaknesses and mistakes, in an ever-so-big way to make the kingdom stride size.

I also grew personally in ways I never dreamed. I became sure about what God has called me to; sensitive to the leading of the Holy Spirit; and steadier in the identity Christ has given me. The new ministry became a place of healing, restoration, and empowerment for me. And that perhaps more than anything else goes to show that when you follow where God's leading —no matter how hard it seems—His blessings are absolutely out of this world.

CONCLUSION

I was joining a new ministry that helped me foster dreams of transition, growth, and a life of deepening trust in God. In the process of looking for and matching with the new relationship and service characteristics, I found the wonderful thing God had for me to live in: part of the vibrant, Christ-centered community.

It reminded me of how important it is to be obedient to the calling of God: though it might be going into an unknown area, the obedience is essential. It also reminded me how God is constantly at work, using every season of our lives to shape us, equip us, and fulfill His purposes. I go to serve in this new ministry with a new sense of purpose and a grateful heart for the journey that God has seen me through. My prayer is that I grow in faith, love, and service so that others may be blessed through the work that God does in and through me.

CHAPTER 6

ACTS OF SERVICE IN MINISTRY

INTRODUCTION

Now that I had found my place in this new ministry, acts of service thrilled me. Acts of service have always been an integral part of my spiritual journey—those ways in which I'm able to concretely express my love for God and for people. What I will present in this chapter includes acts of service that I performed within this ministry and how they affected my faith, the challenges of serving in the Kingdom of God, and the rewards.

THE HEART OF SERVICE

From the very beginning, I knew service must flow from love and humility. Jesus, who washed His disciples' feet, gave the finest example possible of this principle: He showed us that he is the greatest among us who serves. Therefore, I approached my acts of service with a heart bent toward glorifying God in everything that I did and being a blessing to others.

The ministry provided the perfect setting wherein I could serve with the gifts and talents that the Lord had given, whether event planning, mentoring new believers, or helping out where practical needs occurred. In this, I felt a sense of satisfaction in contributing toward the work of the Kingdom. All these acts of service were not simply tasks to be accomplished but opportunities to edify the body of Christ and a way to reflect the love of God.

EMBRACING THE CALL TO SERVE

The first area I got involved with was community outreach. Among the strengths of this church was its concern and outreach to the local community, ministering to spiritual and physical needs. I felt attracted to that kind of ministry because it resonated in my heart for helping those who were marginalized and in dire need.

We organized food drives, clothing donations, and free health clinics with the collaboration of local organizations. I took on a leadership role in coordinating these efforts that demanded a lot of planning and a team-oriented approach. Being able to see tangibly how our collective effort had made a difference in the lives of those whom we served was fulfilling.

Apart from outreach, I volunteered in the church's discipleship program. I had a deep desire to see others grow in Christ, especially new believers who were just starting their journey with Him. I led small groups, facilitated Bible studies, and provided one-on-one mentorship. These relationships were especially dear to my heart because they allowed me to give back to others what was poured into me throughout this journey of faith.

CHALLENGES OF SERVING

Though serving in the ministry was overwhelmingly joyful, it was not without its challenges. Ministries can be very demanding in terms of time, energy, and emotions. At times, it was difficult to juggle all these demands against other responsibilities, and sometimes I even felt stretched thin.

One of the greatest challenges was the maneuvering through the minefield of various personalities and perspectives that were involved with the ministry. Even among believers, misunderstandings can arise. Patience, communication, and humility are some things I have learned about resolving conflicts and working as a team.

There were times when my acts of service went unnoticed or unappreciated. This was a test of motives—was I serving to receive recognition, or was I truly serving for the glory of God? I had to keep telling myself that God sees everything, and it is His approval that would matter most. This mindset kept me focused on the right purpose for which I served.

THE REWARDS OF SERVING

Despite the challenges, the rewards of serving in ministry far outweighed any difficulties. There is something exceptionally fulfilling about knowing you are a part of something much larger than yourself, helping to grow and empower the Kingdom of God. Lives changed, prayers answered, and unity within the body were some of the many strong evidences that kept service fresh in mind.

Perhaps most rewarding of my service were the relationships that were formed along the way. Serving shoulder to shoulder with other men creates a brotherhood that is founded on purpose and mutual support. These were a source of encouragement and strength in serving, particularly during times of challenge or discouragement.

I grew spiritually, too, because of my acts of service. Serving others pushed me out of my comfort zone and stretched my faith. It deepened my reliance on God, as frequently I put myself in situations where His wisdom, strength, and guidance were necessary. Moreover, it kept me grounded with both feet on the ground in relation to the fact that the Christian life is not just about receiving but also giving—giving our time, our resources, and our love.

SERVING IN LOVE AND HUMILITY

Throughout serving in the new ministry, I always tried to remind myself that I am here to serve with love and humility. It wasn't good enough to do good; the attitude and heart behind those works mattered just as much. I strived to serve like Christ did—selflessly, not seeking personal gain or even recognition.

One of the specific verses that helped me was Philippians 2:3-4: "Do nothing out of selfish ambition or vain conceit. Rather, in humility value others above yourselves, not looking to your own interests but each of you to the interests of the others." What this did for me was to challenge myself with regard to my motives every now and then, making sure that what service I was offering was in line with God's will and purpose.

CONCLUSION

Ministry acts of service began to shape my journey with God. In serving, I found the exhilaration that came with contributing to God's work, the struggles that sharpened my character, and profound rewards in lives changing for the better. Service has taught me humility, community, and what it truly means to be a Christ follower.

The more I served, the more I began to realize that everything, no matter how small, is important in advancing the kingdom of God. Whether it be reaching out to the lost, disciplining new believers, or serving the practical needs around us, every act of service reflects God's love and grace. My prayer is to remain faithful to the call to serve, and through my serving, others will be drawn closer to Christ.

These relationships also made room for growth on both ends. By sharing my experiences, I learned from the wisdom and insight of others. This way, through the ideation and support, I grew to maturity in my faith and had so much opened up for me in terms of understanding what it really meant to be part of the body of Christ.

ENTERING INTO SERVICE IN A DIFFERENT WAY

I felt certain ways to get involved as I delved more deeply into that new ministry. My previous experiences put diversified facets of ministry into place, and I was eager to put new settings into practice again with these skills. I did approach the leadership and indicate an interest in contributing, and they welcomed such an interest and were supportive of my involvement.

I started serving in at least a few different capacities and began working with the outreach, discipleship, and worship teams. Each one afforded opportunity to exercise different gifts and develop new ones. New ministry also brought challenges, forcing me to get accustomed to varied styles of leadership, learn new systems, and navigate through different community dynamics. All these challenges were very helpful to the exercise of humility, flexibility, and dependence on God.

Among the most fulfilling aspects of service in this new ministry was seeing God use my past to bless others in the moment. I could use the lessons learned from past challenges and conflicts as tools to help others who might be going through somewhat the same thing. Whether advice, encouragement, or simply a listening ear, I found that God had positioned me well for the moment.

LEARNING TO TRUST GOD IN TRANSITION

Starting a new ministry was such a very critical move in my spiritual journey, and it got to the point of deep trust in God. There were moments of doubt and uncertainty when I questioned whether I had made the right decision. But I kept repeating to myself that God is faithful and that He works everything out for good for those who love Him and are called according to His purpose (Romans 8:28).

This season has brought a teaching for patience, a wait for God's own time. I have learned that transitions are often awkward but make good fertile ground for future great growth. God was really stretching me, pushing past the comfort zones, and teaching me to really learn to depend on Him. In all this, I experienced His provision, guidance, and peace in ways that have served to deepen my faith and trust in Him.

THE FRUIT OF OBEDIENCE

I started seeing the fruit of obedience when I settled into these new ministries. God began to open doors for me to minister among people in ways I had never even imagined. I began to see lives transformed, hearts healed, and people encouraged through this work that God has initiated through my ministry. It's a humbling thing for one to see that the insurmountable God can use one, despite his weaknesses and mistakes, in an ever-so-big way to make the kingdom stride size.

I also grew personally in ways I never dreamed. I became sure about what God has called me to; sensitive to the leading of the Holy Spirit; and steadier in the identity Christ has given me. The new ministry became a place of healing, restoration, and empowerment for me. And that perhaps more than anything else goes to show that when you follow where God's leading —no matter how hard it seems—His blessings are absolutely out of this world.

CONCLUSION

I was joining a new ministry that helped me foster dreams of transition, growth, and a life of deepening trust in God. In the process of looking for and matching with the new relationship and service characteristics, I found the wonderful thing God had for me to live in: part of the vibrant, Christ-centered community.

It reminded me of how important it is to be obedient to the calling of God: though it might be going into an unknown area, the obedience is essential. It also reminded me how God is constantly at work, using every season of our lives to shape us, equip us, and fulfill His purposes. I go to serve in this new ministry with a new sense of purpose and a grateful heart for the journey that God has seen me through. My prayer is that I grow in faith, love, and service so that others may be blessed through the work that God does in and through me.

CHAPTER 7

WALK WITH THE PASTOR

Walking closely with a man of God, even a pastor, can be very rewarding but a complex journey. Having been deeply involved in acts of service within the ministry, I found myself being drawn into an intimate connection with the pastor. This chapter addresses the dynamics, nuances, and lessons taught to me while learning to walk with the pastor in spiritual growth.

THE ROLE OF SPIRITUAL GUIDANCE

I started walking more closely with the man of God—the pastor—with respect for the office. I recognized the shepherd in the form of the pastor as that person whom God had been pleased to lead and guide the flock. Walking more side by side with him was giving me a better understanding of the spiritual dimensions, and I was growing in faith. I hoped to eventually serve and learn from the wisdom cultivated over the years of ministry.

That relationship was, for a while, quite encouraging. The pastor guided me in the faith, counseled me when I needed it, and became my spiritual mentor through the minefields of ministry. There have been times in which there was deep spiritual connection, and the teaching and encouragement of the pastor were uplifting and enabling.

GROWING PAINS AND REALITIES

Over time, though, I began to see the underlying struggles that come with the territory of spiritual leadership in close relationships. To walk with the pastor was to share the internal dynamics of ministry—the victories and the defeats. I saw, before my very eyes, the pressures and burdens associated with a pastoral leader, and it increased my sensitivity to the range of challenges that are part and parcel of being a pastor.

At the same time, this closer proximity brought some tensions to the surface. I began to notice flaws and imperfections in the pastor that I hadn't seen before. It was hard to realize this, as the pastor was put on a pedestal by me; for me, he was almost infallible. But the thing is, pastors, after all, are humans; THEY have their weaknesses and vulnerabilities too.

It forced me to re-evaluate my expectations and how I approached the relationship. It called for grace and more understanding. I learned that spiritual leaders need support, forgiveness, and encouragement like everybody else. That was humbling: really a lesson in how I am supposed to focus on God and not burden any human leader with unrealistic expectations.

DYNAMICS OF POWER AND INFLUENCE

In that connection, it was through walking with the pastor that I learned about power and influence in the church. Getting closer to the pastor, I involved myself increasingly in the various levels of decision-making and leadership discussions. This new influence became very empowering and intimidating. In one way, it made me more suitable to contribute to the ministry, but it has also put me in the crossfire of church politics and the burden of responsibility.

One of such tests was that of walking the tightrope between my loyalty as a congregant to the pastor and my personal inner self-conviction of things. Some occasions found me wrestling within myself over many decisions or directives, which at most times I honestly felt were at variance with my understanding of God's intention. Such moments were particularly hard as I needed to practice unapologetic faith while giving sober respect to the authority of the pastor.

The same power dynamic also set the stage for undue expectations. There was generally an unspoken understanding that those moving closely with the pastor inherently supported the vision or decisions of this figure, despite disagreements with the same. This sometimes caused internal conflicts with me as I sought my own reconciliation between my desire to honor the pastor while being true to myself and remaining authentic to my own convictions.

SERVANT LEADERSHIP VIGNETTES

The walk was hard, but it presented very valuable lessons in servant leadership. I learned that leadership is not about power, control, or administration; it is about serving others in humility and grace. The role of the pastor, when exercised properly, is that of guiding, nurturing, and empowering others toward maturity in faith and the expression of God's purpose upon their lives.

Also, from the experience, I learned to lead by example simply because I watched the effects the pastor's actions and decisions had on the congregation. It made me very cautious about my behavior and exertions upon others. With a sense of leadership, I realized that I did not only owe my people anything, but also that God expected me to be responsible since He had granted me the privilege of leading from the front.

I also learned about the importance of exercising accountability in leadership. Walking with the pastor showed me the importance of having people who act as a support system for others, ready to offer feedback, encouragement, or correction as need be. Accountability safeguards individuals from becoming victim to the pitfalls of pride and staff-induced loneliness prevalent in many leadership positions.

THE IMPACT ON MY SPIRITUAL JOURNEY

Walking with the pastor significantly shaped my spiritual journey, as it increased the value of knowing the complexities of ministry, strengthened my faith, and taught me how to lead in humbleness and grace. It has, on the other hand, therefore been also challenging and trying those very things within my character, patience, and tenacity.

Through this all, I realized that spiritual growth sometimes only happens through adversity and that the Lord uses even hard circumstances to work in and through us. His examples were a reality check on what I might have ignored if I had not gone with the pastor—something that involved much leaning on God and seeking His guidance and an exercise in trust of His plan, even when my plans were not realized.

CONCLUSION

Walking with the pastor was full of blessings and challenges. One could gain insights into how exactly ministry really functions, together with the responsibilities associated with pastoral office, but on the other hand, reflections also revealed complexities and imperfections in human relationship. It was a chapter of moving forward in life that opened my eyes to placing all my trusts in God, extending grace to others, and leading with such humbleness and serving heart.

And so it was that the lessons I picked from walking with the pastor remained within me as I continued the journey on my spiritual path. They would shape my approach to leadership, deepen my compassion toward others, and remind me always to let my eyes be fixed on Jesus, the ultimate shepherd and guide.

CHAPTER 8

A PASTOR'S ROLE AND RESPONSIBILITIES

INTRODUCTION

A person deeply involved in the ministry needs to know what the role and responsibilities of a pastor are. A pastor is viewed as the shepherd over the congregation, called to guide, nurture, and lead the flock in the will of God. In this chapter, I identify, from my observations and experiences in walking closely with one, various roles of a pastor. This was an education that helped me begin to appreciate the weight of pastoral duties and the kind of spiritual, emotional, and practical demands that are put upon leaders in the Church.

THE SPIRITUAL LEADER

Spiritual leadership lies at the heart of a pastor's role. A pastor should be a guide who teaches and preaches the Word of God to the people, providing spiritual nourishment to the congregation. Probably, this is one of the most visible aspects of the role, as much as it has to do with preaching sermons, leading in worship, and administering the sacraments; however, spiritual leadership goes much deeper than the pulpit.

A pastor has to be rooted in prayer and studying the Word to prepare for sermons, but most of all, for one's own spiritual well-being. I have seen how this pastor I walked with often spent hours in solitude, seeking God's direction and even interceding for the congregation. This is another spiritual discipline that was an integral component—because a pastor needs sensitivity to the leading of the Holy Spirit if he were to lead effectively.

Moreover, a pastor ought to be an example in living according to the teachings of Christ. This will mean there is so much that is expected of him by the congregation, who looks to the pastor for spiritual inspiration and guidance. Indeed, I was able to note how the personal walk of God that was exhibited by the pastor influenced the spiritual atmosphere of the church. When the pastor was strong spiritually, so was the church; when the pastor was weak, so was the church.

THE SHEPHERD AND CAREGIVER

Another very important attribute about a pastor's role is that of being a shepherd and caregiver. This includes offering pastoral care to the congregation, such as the comforting of those who have suffered a loss, counseling the troubled, visiting the sick, and supporting people in crisis. The pastor has to be sensitive to the needs of the congregation, which calls for offering care, wisdom, and practical assistance where needed.

What touched me the most was the commitment of the pastor to this position. There were numerous times the pastor canceled personal plans to tend to a member of the congregation. From the visit to the hospital to sit with a family, through marriage counseling, to praying with someone through a difficult decision, the pastor brought comfort and strength in his presence to many.

This is an emotionally draining part of pastoral ministry. A pastor literally carries a congregation on their shoulders, weeping with those who weep and rejoicing with those who rejoice. That takes a full wellspring of empathy, patience, and resilience. I learned that though the pastor is present to support others, they, too, need to be supported—either from other leaders within the church, trusted friends, or a personal counselor.

THE ADMINISTRATOR AND VISIONARY

A pastor is not only a spiritual leader and caregiver but also a church administrator and visionary. The position calls for overseeing daily operations of the church and handling its staff members and volunteers. It also includes financial management and ensures that the various ministries of the churches are running smoothly. It also involves vision-casting for the future of the church, setting of goals, and guiding and leading the congregation to the achievement of mission.

I was most surprised by the amount of time and energy that the administrative side of pastoral work took: organizing events, leading meetings, managing conflicts, making a great number of decisions that involved the whole church—it all not only took organizational skills but also delegation and collaboration with others.

Another critical part of a pastor's role is being a visionary. A pastor should seek God's direction for the church, knowing where the congregation is called and how to lead them in that process. This demands spiritual discernment and strategic planning. In this context, I have observed how frequently the pastor gathers leaders and members to pray and talk through the direction of the church, therefore creating unity and purpose.

CHALLENGES AND PRESSURES

The role of a pastor is not free from challenges and pressures. Probably the most difficult is being expected to be all things to all people. Congregants look to the pastor as spiritual leader but also as counselor, mediator, teacher, and administrator. Balancing these varied roles can be overwhelming when, at the same time, there are all the personal problems that each individual encounters.

The pressure to live up to the image or standard set can sometimes be very strong. Pastors are generally expected to be paragons of virtue: always strong in faith, wise in decisions, and patient in demeanor. This potentially creates isolation, as pastors may find it hard to find safe spaces where they can become vulnerable and find support.

I saw how these pressures could wear down the pastor I walked with. At times, the weight of responsibility he carried was almost unbearable. It became evident that the pastor's role is far from a job but a calling—one that entails dependence on God and support from the community.

THE NEED FOR PERSONAL CARE AND ACCOUNTABILITY

With responsibilities and pressures so great, it becomes imperative that any pastor care for himself and be accountable. A pastor has to keep physically, emotionally, and spiritually fit if he is to be an effective pastor. This means time to rest, personal spiritual exercises, and seeking help as necessary.

As important as all these things is the issue of accountability. Pastors need a network of trusted others—a mentor, a counselor, or a peer group—to whom they can turn for counsel, encouragement, and correction. It will avert burnout, promote integrity, and keep one's feet on the ground regarding one's calling.

What I saw was this: when the pastor is not taking care of himself, he is affecting his well-being and functionality in the ministry. In contrast, when the pastor took rest, prayed, and measures of accountability were in place, the church benefited by receiving a healthier, more energized leader.

CONCLUSION

The pastor's task is manifold. A pastor should be a spiritual leader, shepherd, caregiver, administrator, and visionary. This call will require much in the way of spiritual maturity, strength of mind, and commitment to serving God and His people. It will also press upon a person a series of challenging pressures, battering even the most dedicated pastor.

It was in this walk with a pastor that I truly came to appreciate how heavy pastoral ministry could be. Informed by this principle, whereas pastors are called to lead, so they themselves need support, encouragement, and care. Most importantly, what I learned from pastoral ministry is this: it is not one of questionably taking up roles and responsibilities but one in which one answers God's call to serve faithfully, trusting in His strength and guidance throughout.

CHAPTER 9

MY DAVID & SAUL EXPERIENCE & CONFLICTS IN MINISTRY

The Bible itself, in the relationship between David and Saul, got a very powerful metaphor of describing conflicts in ministry. The story of King Saul's jealousy and subsequent enmity toward David, who was anointed to become his successor, shows the agonizing tensions that can arise during the transfer of God's anointing in leadership. Chain reactions can come into play just like dominoes, resulting in conflicts in ministry that can prove a real working-out trial of faith, patience, and commitment to the way God has pointed out.

1. DAVID'S ANOINTING

While Saul was reigning, God had chosen David as the future king of Israel. The divine selection of David formed a moment that would lead to future conflict. There are those times in ministry when God's favor and anointing rest visibly on someone new; this can create tension with those who are then in leadership. In many ways, it's not about the failures of the current leader but rather God and his timing.

2. THE JEALOUSY AND FEAR OF SAUL

As David began to increase in prominence, so did the jealousy of Saul. Saul recognized anointing upon the life of David and feared he would possibly lose his throne and favor with the people. In a ministry context, this can mean that the rising leader who manifests gifts, talents, and anointing will create feelings of threat to the established leader. The result of this fear can be actions aimed at guarding one's position rather than serving God's people.

3. DAVID'S RESPECT FOR SAUL

Despite the growing hostility of the relationship, David continued to respect and honor Saul, even refusing to harm him when opportunity came his way. This is an important part of the David and Saul story for anyone experiencing conflict in ministry. Indeed, David acted humbly, with patience, and in full trust in God's timing. He knew that God's plan would unfold in His way and in His time, and that taking things into one's own hands was not glorifying God.

4. THE BATTLE INTENSIFIES

The conflict had only just begun, though, for as Saul's jealousy became full-blown persecution. David was forced to flee and live as a fugitive because of Saul's seeking his life. Conflicts can sometimes get that bad in ministry, and reconciliation may seem impossible; one party may even feel forced to leave or step down. This is very painful and can bring deep emotional and spiritual wounds.

5. TRUSTING GOD IN THE MIDST OF CONFLICT

David's story was one of trusting God in the midst of turmoil. His relentlessness to seek God amidst all the pressure and danger meant David did not return a blow to Saul but continued patiently to let God be the judge. Trusting God can sometimes be very difficult in ministry when opposition occurs, especially when it seems so undeserved or unwarranted. Yet, in the case of David, experience taught him God is faithful, and no man's hand can stop what God intends to do.

6. THE TEMPTATION TO FIGHT BACK

There were indeed occasions when David could have taken the opportunity to fight back, take things into his hands, and seize what looked rightfully his. But he did not go that far as he knew by doing so, he would be acting outside of the will of God. In many ministry conflicts as well, there is this temptation at the same time to be able to strike back—the temptation to protect oneself from attack or to assertively claim one's rightful place and, if necessary, to take it by force as he believes it to have been divinely called upon for. However, David's example teaches that true leadership in God's kingdom is characterized by constraint, humility, and respect for God's timing.

7. THE ROLE OF MENTORSHIP

Arguably, Saul began as a mentor to David, inviting him into his court and giving him responsibilities. This relationship, however, fell apart as jealousy set in. In this one respect, their story could be understood to mean the importance of mentorship in ministry and how it can either build or destroy. For the leaders among them, this involves the task of educating future leaders, but with generosity in spirit, allowing God to do whatever He desires, even if it means moving over for Him.

8. HEALING AND FORGIVENESS

Even though the story of David and Saul did not go well, culminating in the death of Saul, the reaction by David to Saul's death was telling. He wept for Saul and treated him with respect despite all that had happened. More often than not, the response underlines the need for forgiveness and healing within ministerial conflicts. Bitterness and resentment are spiritually damning. Healing actually occurs through forgiving those who offended us and trusting God to bring justice and restoration.

9. LEARNING FROM THE EXPERIENCE

David's experiences with Saul were not only a period of suffering but of preparation. These trials shaped him into the king he would become. The conflicts within the ministry can serve as a refining fire, teaching many needed lessons about leadership, faith, and dependence upon God. Conflicts should not be viewed as entirely negative but as opportunities for growth and deeper dependence upon God.

10. GRACE TO MOVE ON

Following the death of Saul, David now became the king, as God promised. He did so graciously, with no desire to seek revenge from some who had stood against him earlier. Instead, he moved into the leadership for his people. Similarly, in ministry, there should be graceful moving forward after conflicts have been resolved and settled, focusing on the future rather than lingering over past hurts. Only then can healing take place and God's calling be fulfilled.

CONCLUSION (EMBRACING GOD'S SOVEREIGNTY)

God's total dependence can be thoroughly appreciated and best experienced through the story of David and Saul, even when pertains to the ministry. They are really unexpected in the majority of cases, and of course, offending. However, the posture of humility, trust, and obedience towards God will enable one to walk with God through the conflicts, just like David, so life ways may be honored before God, and one's life suits God and His intentions. It is through such experiences that God often prepares us for greater responsibilities and deeper levels of service in his kingdom.

CHAPTER 10

THE OFFENSES CAME

Offenses in the context of church or ministry are bound to happen and are generally difficult. An offense can come for any or no reason. It is vital to recognize and deal with such offenses with grace and wisdom for the sake of unity and the health of the life community. The chapter deals with the nature of the offences, their impact on relations and ministries, practical steps towards dealing with and resolving them.

UNDERSTANDING THE NATURE OF OFFENSES

Offenses in ministry are mainly results from unmet expectations, miscommunication, and personal conflicts. They at times may start as small issues but end up being major problems if not resolved on time. In this case, understanding the nature of these offenses means that offenses are an integral part of human interaction and the life of ministry. Everybody, at one time, will either cause offense or be offended.

1. **Misunderstandings**: Sometimes simple miscommunications snowball into big, battling conflicts. Most of these happen either because expectations were not clearly given or because someone interprets someone else's actions or words based on one's own prejudices.

2. **Different Expectations**: People come into the ministry with varied expectations and goals in mind. If these are not aligned, it can be a source for disappointment and conflict.

3. **Personal Grievances**: Past hurts and unresolved issues are what dictate reactions to things in the church. Such personal grievances increase conflicts, leading to offenses.

THE IMPACT OF OFFENSES ON RELATIONSHIPS

Offenses, when they do occur, have deep effects on relationships within the church. It is important to understand such impacts as a means to address and heal the wounds that offenses cause.

1. **Erosion of trust**: Offenses can cause strained relationships between two people, making it hard for them to work together or for them to be in a healthy relationship. Trust is very fundamental in the ministry, and when it is broken, rebuilding takes time and a lot of effort.

2. **Emotional Distress**: Those offended might undergo emotional distress, which may range from anger, hurt, or resentment. These emotions might stand in the way of their wellness and good actions within the ministry.

3. **Division and Conflict**: Offenses can create a division in the church, whereby factions or cliques end up working for things that are opposed to unity and togetherness. This division can be very harmful to a community that thrives on acting in togetherness and helping each other.

DEALING WITH OFFENSES CONSTRUCTIVELY

Dealing with offenses constructively becomes very critical in handling the restoration of relationships and a healthy atmosphere in the church. The following are some practical ways of dealing with offenses:

1. **Understand**: Whenever there is an offense, understand the other person's perspective. Communicate openly and honestly, and listen actively and empathetically to their concerns and feelings.

2. **Acknowledge and Apologize**: Do so if you are the offender. Acknowledge your mistake and apologize sincerely. It means much more than saying "I am sorry." Apologizing requires that you not only be responsible but also seek to mend things.

3. **Forgive and Let Go**: It is relevant to healing because by forgiving somebody who you might think offended you, you make a conscious decision not to stay with the hurt and resentment. It does not mean one condones the offense, but it means one moves on without letting the offense determine what one does.

4. **Work Towards Reconciliation**: Reconciliation is when both parties resume a healthy relationship. This process may be long-term and include setting new boundaries to begin rebuilding trust. However, patience and persistence are expected in the course of working through the process.

5. **Mediation**: In a few circumstances, although it might be necessary, it might be of some value for both parties to approach a mediator, an independent person that can help two other people resolve a dispute. Mediation should encourage both parties to communicate with each other, clarify any misunderstanding, and begin the process of reconciliation.

PREVENTION OF FURTHER OFFENSES

While it's not possible to eliminate all potential for offense, there are ways to minimize the occurrence and impact.

1. **Foster open communication**: Encourage an open and honest communication environment. Regularly check in with them to team members and fellow congregants in a bid to ensure clarity on expectations and issues—should any arise—to be resolved on time.

2. **Set clear expectations**: Articulate the roles, responsibilities, and expectations operating within the ministry. It eliminates misconceptions and keeps everyone on the same page.

3. **Cultivate Respect**: Develop an attitude and culture of respect and understanding when it comes to differing opinions and perspectives. Empathy and considerations in all interactions should be encouraged.

4. **Provide Training and Resources**: Here, training in conflict resolution, good communication, and emotional intelligence will help to give people the tools they need to understand the way they should get along and resolve conflicts.

THE ROLE OF LEADERSHIP IN HANDLING OFFENSES

Leadership is one of the crucial aspects in the process of addressing or dealing with offenses in church. They are to give the agenda on how conflicts are to be dealt with and take their congregations in hard times.

1. **Model Grace and Humility**: Leaders are to model grace and humility in their own interactions. By showing others how to constructively handle offenses, it becomes a very powerful example.

2. **Assure Accountability**: Make sure all members of the church are held responsible for their actions. Fairly and consistently address issues; support people who are trying to work through conflicts.

3. **Heal and Restore**: Heal and restore, rather than punish or seek retribution. Help people deal with forgiveness and reconciliation.

MOVING FORWARD

Once an offense has been addressed, one moves forward, recommitting to a vision of unity and working together. The objective is not to dredge up past hurts but to build better relationships and a more robust community.

1. **Acknowledge the Achievements**: Appreciate and celebrate the progress made in working towards the resolution of conflicts and restoration of relationships. Such a mechanism of reinforcement will help confirm the positive behaviors and create a sense of community.

2. **Continue to Build Trust**: Keep working towards building and maintaining trust within the church. Trust is built through consistent actions that are seen, through transparent communication, and through a sincere commitment toward conflict resolution in healthy ways.

3. **Mission-focused**: Keep the mission and vision of the church in clear focus. Movement toward common goals will help to overcome past friction and move forward in a certain sense of purpose.

CONCLUSION (EMBRACING THE JOURNEY)

Offenses are an inherent part of ministry and community life. How we deal with them will either strengthen or weaken our relationships and our ministry. Handling offenses graciously, sensitively, and recognizing the need to reconcile may build more strength for a community that finds itself in such experiences. Acceptance of the journey of conflict resolution, for the purpose of healing and unity, must therefore be to the glory of God and be seen to stand up for each other in our common mission.

CHAPTER 11

THE REJECTION CAME

Rejection has got to be one of the most painful things to ever encounter, especially in the ministry, since there are relationships, acceptance, and community involved. That rejection can break down the very confidence in yourself, your faith, and even your sense of purpose. Being rejected is a part of life, but how one handles it can possibly shape where you are headed in life most times. This chapter scrapes the nature of rejection, the impact on the people and ministries, and how to come out of the deep slick with grace and resilience.

UNDERSTANDING THE NATURE OF REJECTION

Rejection, in a ministry context, may come in various forms, such as exclusion from a group, being disregarded, ideas criticized, or laid off from work. It generally feels personal and can merely be the onset of deep emotional hurts. Understanding the nature of rejection is the first step in dealing with it effectively.

1. **Rejection as a Part of Life:** Rejection is an experience that cannot be averted in life and ministry. Nobody is exempt, not even the most successful leaders or ministers who have ever walked the earth. It, therefore, helps to center the situation concerning the understanding that rejection is something every person faces.

2. **The Role of Expectations:** Sometimes, our expectations will amplify the pain of rejection. If we happen to expect acceptance, approval, or success and that does not take place, the rejection which follows does seem to go much deeper. It is possible to manage expectations in such a way as to enable us to handle the pain better.

3. **Rejection within the Bible:** Rejection is throughout the Bible-from Joseph's brothers, who sold him into slavery, to David pursued by Saul, to Jesus Who was rejected by His people. The setups that were set up for fulfillment became those things that brought rejection. These stories remind us that rejection often is not the end of the story but rather a step toward greater purpose.

THE EMOTIONAL AND SPIRITUAL IMPACT OF REJECTION

Both emotional and spiritual aspects are in jeopardy because of rejection. Worthlessness, isolation, and doubt are some of the common feelings that are provoked because of rejection. However, identification of these impacts is the first step back to healing and recovery.

1. **Emotional Pain**: Emotional pain because of rejection may come in the form of pain, anger, or depression. These facts must be acknowledged and not stored. Storing these feelings will result in further damage.

   Spiritual doubt-the rejection may develop in one a feeling of doubt about their calling, their worth, and even God's plan for them. You may wonder why God would let you go through such pain, but it is important that you hold on to your faith at this time.

2. **Loss of confidence in self**: Rejections, if consistent, can destroy your confidence altogether. Most times, you would not be willing to go out in faith or take any dicey venture anymore. Your self-confidence needs time to rebuild, but it's a bridge toward the next steps of life.

HOW TO RESPOND TO REJECTION WITH GRACE

How you respond to rejection can determine whether or not it will serve as a stepping stone or a stumbling block. Responding with grace means standing in your integrity, trusting God's plan, and learning from it.

1. **Go to God**: these moments of rejection are when you should go to God in prayer and meditation. Derive comfort in His presence and divine guidance in His Word. Remember that the acceptance by God is unconditional and eternal.

2. **Forgive and Let Go**: Forgiveness is what will heal the rejection you have gone through. Holding on to bitterness or animosity will only prolong your agony. Forgive those who rejected you and let the whole situation go off to God, across the universe.

3. **Seek Support:** Do not keep to yourself in isolation because of the pain. Reach out to trustworthy friends, mentors, or counselors who can offer support and perspective. Sharing your experience with others will help you process your feelings and gain insight into ways you might grow from it.

4. **Learn and Grow**: Every experience of rejection carries with it the potential for growth. Reflect on what can be learned from the situation. Perhaps you need to grow in those areas identified, or maybe the rejection is acting as a form of redirection for something better.

OVERCOMING THE FEAR OF REJECTION

That fear is crippling and will hold you back from taking a chance or stepping into something new. Overcoming this is crucial for the realization of what you're supposed to do and living that out.

Develop Resilience: It's the aspect of bouncing back from setbacks. Resilience is built through developing the right mindset and staying connected with your purpose, never letting rejection define you.

1. **Be Vulnerable:** This means opening oneself up to risk-even rejection. Being OK with rejection is what embracing vulnerability means; it should not hold you back from achieving what you want.

2. **Focus on God's Path:** Remember, as immortalised in this God-gathered path, His plan for your life is bigger than any other rejection you can possibly be given. Be sure that God is leading you and, through the rejections, He will direct you into His perfect will.

3. **Take Action:** Do not let the fear of rejection make you inactive. The more you chase that new ministry, share your ideas, or hang out with someone, the faster it goes away.

REJECTION AS A REDIRECTION

Very often, rejection turns out to be a kind of needed, wholesome redirection. God can close that door but open another, a direction where you need to go more in line with your gifts and calling.

1. **Patience with God's Timing:** His timing is perfect, despite our timing. Trust that the delays and rejections that are by Him are meaningful and take you to the right place at the right time.

2. **Look for New Opportunities:** Most times, rejection clears the path to new opportunities you might have never considered. Be open to where God may be leading you next.

3. **Reframe the Experience:** Instead of looking at rejection as a failure, reframe it as an opportunity for growth and redirection. What lessons can you take from the experience? How can you use it to better align with God's plan for your life?

MOVING FORWARD AFTER REJECTION

Rejection is the call for a new sense of purpose and resolve as you proceed in your life and calling. With this understanding, you should never allow rejection to do much damage to your pursuit of your calling any more.

1. **Refocus on Your Calling**: Always remind yourself of the high and holy calling you are called upon and why you were brought into the ministry. It will help you rekindle your flame and refocus once more.

2. **Set New Goals**: Take the rejection as an opportunity to fix yourself new goals and seek new opportunities. May it be in learning new skills, embarking on a new ministry service, or just in getting to know your God in a fresher, deeper way, new goals can guide you into the future.

3. **Be Positive**: Maintain a positive attitude. Keep close to your heart the good part of life and ministry. Worry about the future instead of nursing bitterness after rejections.

4. **Move on**: You never get caught in time because of rejection. Move on, fully convinced that God is with you. Long steps forward are steps toward healing, growing, and being in the fullness of your God-ordained purpose.

CONCLUSION (EMBRACING GOD'S PLAN)

Rejection hurts, but it is not the end of the journey. Rejection is part of the journey that will bring further growth, more character, and more compliance with the will of God for your life. You can respond to rejection with grace, trusting God's redirection, and moving with purpose forward. Perhaps in so doing, you could transcend the hurt of rejection into the fullness of what God has for you. Enjoy the journey, for every rejection means you are a step closer to the perfect will of God for your life.

CHAPTER 12

FALSE HUMILITY, FALSE LOVE

In ministry, there are often two primary assumed virtues that are foundational: humility and love. Yet often, these very virtues are misunderstood, misrepresented, and even manipulated. Where humility and love are performed but not an expression from the heart, they are rendered impotent and unreal. This chapter shall discuss the nature of false humility and false love, how they impact ministry, and also how to cultivate true humility and love in your life.

THE NATURE OF TRUE HUMILITY AND LOVE

Before dealing with the issue of false humility and false love, it would be appropriate to say something about what true humility and love are. True humility and love find their deepest foundation in the character of Christ, being indispensable to any ministry that is to be healthy and productive.

1. **True Humility:** True humility is not thinking less of yourself but thinking of yourself less. It is an honest recognition of your strengths and weaknesses, coupled with the readiness to serve others without expectation of recognition or praise. Humility places others before oneself not because one feels oneself to be inferior to others but because he/she genuinely wants to help others grow and thrive.

2. **True Love:** It is selfless, unconditional, and sacrificial. True love pursues the interests of another with no concern about personal loss. Love within ministry is not pretending, caring for people without an ulterior motive. Love is patient, kind, and never envious or boastful. True love becomes the prime mover for all ministry that counts.

THE DANGERS OF FALSE HUMILITY

It is called false humility, but it does not always bear that appearance at first glance; rather, it may masquerade as true humility. It is rooted, though, in pride and insecurity rather than a genuine desire to serve others.

1. **Approval Seeking**: So many times, false humility stems from the need for approval or the need to feel validated through other people's approval. As opposed to serving out of a pure heart, a person with false humility will more often than not minimize their own abilities or successes in order to get some reassuring praise or assurance from someone else. It is manipulative and really self-serving.

2. **Disguised Pride**: Sometimes, false humility is pride disguised. Constant deprecation about oneself or refusing to accept compliments might be subtler ways of drawing attention toward one's self and making it all about one's perceived humility rather than being about others.

3. **Lacking responsibility**: Some of the pseudo-humilities are when a person does not want to take responsibility or lead, saying that the person is not "worthy" or "capable." This is the excuse for not taking charge in circumstances that demand one's presence-it hampers the work of the ministry, therefore.

IDENTIFYING AND REJECTING FALSE HUMILITY

Both recognizing and overcoming false humility require honesty and introspection of oneself or others. Overcoming requires a commitment to true humility, which is anchored in servanthood that is Christ-like.

1. **Personal Examination**: Regularly question your motives for serving others and relating to them. Are you desiring recognition, approval, or vindication? Are you evading responsibility because of an appearance of humility? Honesty with oneself is the first step towards true humility.

2. **Exercise Your Gifts**: True humility recognizes God's gifts and talents in your life, and puts them into practice for His glory, rather than hiding or minimizing them. Embrace your strengths and use them in serving others, giving credit to God for all you accomplish.

3. **Serve without expectation**: Practice serving others without expecting anything in return-not even recognition or gratitude. This helps to take the spotlight off of yourself and onto the needs of others.

THE DANGERS OF FALSE LOVE

Equally hazardous in ministry is false love. It's love that expects something in return, or is self-serving, or manipulative. It may look real on the surface, but it doesn't have the richness and genuineness of true Christ-like love.

1. **Conditional Love:** Typically, fake love has strings attached to it. It is always given for the expectation of gaining something in return, be it loyalty, affection, or compliance. Rather than being selfless, this kind of love is transactional and gives rise to an unnatural dynamic within relationships.

   Manipulative love involves using such love to manipulate through guilt complex feelings, emotional blackmail, or a situation where one has control through a display of love and affection in order to get others to do something for their benefit. Manipulative love is never about the well-being of another person but about what one might get from them.

2. **The Superficial Love**: The false love is shallow and superficial, being more concerned with the superficial aspects than the actual care. This may point toward the execution of motions that are regarded as loving actions, such as giving compliments or performing acts of kindness, without actual concern or compassion to back up the action.

FOSTERING A GENUINE LOVE

Genuine love is the substance of any serious ministry. It means deep commitment to the welfare of others based on the love of Christ.

1. **Check your motives**: Periodically take a personal inventory of your motives for showing love to others. Is it genuinely to take care of them, or do you have an ulterior motive? Ask God to cleanse your heart and motives.

2. **Practice sacrificial love**: True love is often sacrificial in nature. It is about putting other people's needs above your own—even at the cost of inconvenience or when it costs you something. Be on the lookout for ways to love others sacrificially, not looking for anything in return.

3. **Build deep relationships**: Shallow love cannot stand the tests of ministry. Create deep, authentic relationships with the people around you. Be vulnerable and honest, committed to walking alongside others through their struggles.

THE IMPACT OF FALSE HUMILITY AND FALSE LOVE ON MINISTRY

It can easily be understood that false humility and false love in ministry will bring two results: inappropriate relationships, mistrust, and a lack of true community.

1. **Eroding trust:** When people feel that your humility or love is fake, the trust will be eroded. They may start doubting your real intentions and may tend to keep a distance that could see the unity and effectiveness of your ministry shattered.

2. **Creating Division**: False humility and love are ways that often bring about division in a ministry because members feel manipulated, cast aside, or deceived. It can lead to conflicts, resentments, and the breakdown of relationships.

3. **Hindering God's Work**: In the final analysis, false humility and false love create hindrances to the work of God in and through your ministry. These virtues, when not authentic, can be barriers to the work of the Holy Spirit—barriers against real transformation and growth.

EMBRACING TRUE HUMILITY AND LOVE IN MINISTRY

It should never be overemphasized that true humility and love are at the core of any ministry and must be so if it is to be a ministry like that of Jesus' life and ministry.

1. **Follow the Example of Christ**: Jesus is the greatest example of true humility and love. He humbled himself, even to the death of the cross, and then loved others selflessly and unconditionally. Strive to follow His example into your ministry and life.

2. **Seek Accountability**: Surround yourself with people who can hold you accountable in your journey towards genuine humility and love. You can have a trustworthy friend, mentor, or spiritual adviser who will help you be true to these virtues and not make you slip into counterfeit humility and love.

3. **Pray for Transformation:** Pray that God would transform your heart and mind, so that your humility and love would be real reflections of God's character. Through regular prayer and time in God's Word, you will stay in line with His will.

   Let your commitment be to live a life of integrity in the ministry. Let all your actions, words, and attitudes reflect the true humility and love that false virtue talks about. In this way, you will be able to earn their trust, forge much-needed relationships, and provide that essential bedrock on which to build your powerful ministry.

CONCLUSION: THE POWER OF AUTHENTIC VIRTUE

The two devils which work hand in hand to destroy God's work in ministry are false humility and false love. These lead to division, un-trust, and the absence of true community. But where humility and love are real, they can take the kingdom and use the strongest of tools to build it. Following in Christ's steps, seeking accountability, praying for transformation-these will help you have true humility and love in life and in your ministry. Then God will work and bring the drama to completion.

This chapter makes more assertion on the sincerity of humility and love, warning against their false forms, and encourages a Christ-centered orientation in ministry.

Don't let rejection stop you in your tracks. Keep moving on, with the faith that God is with you every step you take. Each step taken forward is a step towards healing, growth, and fulfilling your God-given purpose.

CHAPTER 13

FORGIVING THE OFFENDER

Forgiveness is one of the most challenging yet essential virtues in the Christian faith. In ministry, offenses will inevitably come—whether through misunderstandings, betrayal, or intentional harm. Forgiving the offender is not just a recommendation; it is a command that stems from the heart of God. This chapter delves into the importance of forgiveness, the process of forgiving those who have hurt you, and the freedom that comes from releasing bitterness and embracing reconciliation.

THE BIBLICAL MANDATE FOR FORGIVENESS

Forgiveness is at the core of the Gospel message. Jesus Christ, through His sacrificial death on the cross, extended forgiveness to all who believe in Him. This act of grace and mercy sets the standard for how we are to treat others, especially those who have wronged us.

1. **Jesus' Teachings on Forgiveness:** In the Gospels, Jesus repeatedly emphasized the importance of forgiveness. In Matthew 6:14-15, He states, "For if you forgive others their trespasses, your heavenly Father will also forgive you, but if you do not forgive others their trespasses, neither will your Father forgive your trespasses." This passage underscores the reciprocal nature of forgiveness; our willingness to forgive others is directly connected to our experience of God's forgiveness.

2. **Parable of the Unforgiving Servant:** In Matthew 18:21-35, Jesus tells the parable of the unforgiving servant to illustrate the consequences of withholding forgiveness. A servant who was forgiven a great debt by his master refused to forgive a fellow servant who owed him a small amount. The master, upon hearing

this, punished the unforgiving servant, showing that those who have been forgiven much must also forgive others.

3. **Forgiveness is Not Optional:** Forgiveness is not merely a suggestion for believers; it is a command. As followers of Christ, we are called to extend the same grace and mercy to others that we have received from God. Forgiveness is a non-negotiable aspect of Christian living and ministry.

THE NATURE OF FORGIVENESS

Understanding what forgiveness is—and what it is not—is crucial for any believer. Forgiveness is often misunderstood, and these misconceptions can hinder our ability to forgive.

1. **Forgiveness is a Choice, Not a Feeling**: Many people wait to feel like forgiving someone, but forgiveness is a conscious decision, not an emotion. It is an act of the will, often in spite of lingering feelings of hurt or anger. You may not feel like forgiving, but by choosing to do so, you align yourself with God's will.

2. **Forgiveness is Not Forgetting**: The phrase "forgive and forget" can be misleading. Forgiving does not mean that you erase the memory of the offense. Instead, it means choosing not to hold the offense against the person. It's about letting go of the desire for revenge and trusting God to handle the justice.

3. **Forgiveness is Not Excusing the Offense**: Forgiveness does not mean that the offense was acceptable or that it should be ignored. It is not condoning the wrong or dismissing the need for accountability. Forgiveness can coexist with justice, as it involves releasing the offender to God's judgment rather than seeking personal retribution.

4. **Forgiveness is a Process**: While forgiveness is a decision, it often involves a process, especially for deep or repeated wounds. It may require time, prayer, and continual surrender to God. Each step of choosing forgiveness allows God to heal the broken places in your heart.

THE BENEFITS OF FORGIVING THE OFFENDER

Forgiveness is not only beneficial to the offender; it is also immensely liberating for the one who forgives. The act of forgiving can bring about profound healing and freedom.

1. **Emotional and Spiritual Freedom:** Unforgiveness is like a prison that keeps you bound in bitterness, anger, and resentment. Choosing to forgive releases you from that prison and brings emotional and spiritual freedom. It allows you to move forward without being weighed down by the past.

2. **Healing and Restoration**: Forgiveness is a key component of healing, both for the offended and the offender. It opens the door for restoration and reconciliation, although it doesn't always guarantee it. Even if reconciliation doesn't occur, forgiveness brings inner peace and healing.

3. **Breaks the Cycle of Pain:** Holding onto unforgiveness often perpetuates a cycle of pain, causing ongoing harm to relationships, families, and communities. Forgiveness breaks this cycle and creates an opportunity for new beginnings, healthier relationships, and a more loving community.

4. **Aligns Us with God's Will**: When we forgive, we align ourselves with God's will and reflect His character. It strengthens our relationship with Him and keeps our hearts soft and receptive to His guidance.

PRACTICAL STEPS TO FORGIVING THE OFFENDER

Forgiveness, while essential, is not always easy. Here are some practical steps to help you in the journey of forgiving those who have hurt you:

1. **Acknowledge the Pain**: Start by acknowledging the pain and hurt caused by the offender. Denying or minimizing the hurt only leads to unresolved emotions. Be honest with yourself and with God about how you feel.

2. **Pray for God's Help**: Forgiveness often requires divine intervention. Ask God for the strength, grace, and willingness to forgive. Pray for healing in your heart and for the offender as well.

Sometimes, praying for those who have hurt you can soften your heart toward them.

3. **Release the Offense to God**: Choose to release the offense and the offender to God. This means letting go of the desire for revenge or justice on your terms and trusting God to handle the situation. It may help to write down the offense and symbolically release it by tearing up the paper or burning it.

4. **Seek Support and Counsel**: Sometimes, forgiveness is difficult to navigate alone. Seek support from trusted friends, mentors, or counselors who can provide guidance and encouragement. They can help you process your emotions and keep you accountable in your journey toward forgiveness.

5. **Set Healthy Boundaries**: Forgiving someone does not mean allowing them to continue hurting you. It's important to set healthy boundaries to protect yourself from further harm. Boundaries can help maintain the integrity of your forgiveness while also ensuring your well-being.

6. **Take One Day at a Time**: Forgiveness can be a daily choice, especially in cases of deep hurt or repeated offenses. Take it one day at a time, relying on God's grace to help you forgive. Over time, you will find that the pain lessens and the freedom grows.

THE ROLE OF RECONCILIATION IN FORGIVENESS

While forgiveness is an internal process, reconciliation involves both parties and requires mutual effort and willingness. Not all forgiveness leads to reconciliation, but when it does, it can be a beautiful testimony of God's grace.

1. **Reconciliation Requires Repentance**: For true reconciliation to occur, the offender must acknowledge their wrongdoing, repent, and seek to make amends. Without genuine repentance, reconciliation may not be possible, even though forgiveness is.

2. **Reconciliation is a Journey**: Just like forgiveness, reconciliation is often a journey that takes time, effort, and patience. It involves rebuilding trust, which may have been broken by the offense. Both

parties must be committed to the process and be willing to work through the challenges.

3. **Forgiveness Without Reconciliation:** In some cases, reconciliation may not be possible or healthy, especially if the offender is unrepentant or the offense was particularly harmful. In such situations, it is still important to forgive, but reconciliation should be approached with wisdom and discernment.

THE EXAMPLE OF CHRIST: THE ULTIMATE FORGIVER

Jesus Christ is our ultimate example of forgiveness. Even as He hung on the cross, suffering for the sins of humanity, He prayed, "Father, forgive them, for they do not know what they are doing" (Luke 23:34). His willingness to forgive, even in the face of unimaginable pain and betrayal, sets the standard for how we are to forgive those who offend us.

1. **Following Christ's Example**: When we forgive, we follow in the footsteps of Christ. We become more like Him and demonstrate His love and grace to a world in desperate need of it. Our forgiveness becomes a powerful witness to the transformative power of the Gospel.

2. **Forgiveness as Worship:** Forgiveness is not just an act of obedience; it is an act of worship. When we forgive, we honor God and acknowledge His sovereignty over our lives. We surrender our right to retaliate and trust that He is a just and righteous judge.

CONCLUSION (FORGIVENESS AS FREEDOM)

Forgiving the offender is not easy, but it is necessary for our spiritual growth, emotional healing, and effective ministry. It liberates us from the chains of bitterness, resentment, and anger, allowing us to live in the freedom that Christ has promised. By choosing to forgive, we reflect the heart of God and create an environment where His love, grace, and mercy can flow freely. May we always remember that just as we have been forgiven much, we are called to forgive others with the same measure of grace and mercy.

CHAPTER 14

MOVING ON BY FAITH

The principle of moving on by faith is applicable to all believers who have been in some kind of hurt, disappointment, or discouragement sometime in their ministry journey. Just as life is, so ministry is also beset with many ups and downs that may discourage even the most devoted servant of God from continuing His work. But, faith is what enables one to rise above it and to press on, continuing the work God has called us into. It considers the need to believe in moving on, practical ways of getting back after falling, and God's promises, which put some hope for the future.

THE NATURE OF FAITH IN MOVING FORWARD

Faith is not just a mental assent or wishful thinking; it is a deep trust and reliance upon God whereby one shapes life in going forward.

Faith in God's sovereignty is the bedrock upon which to move forward by faith. It requires trusting God when circumstances would indicate anything but He is in control. It is here where trust is rooted in understanding that God works all things together for the good of those who love Him and are called according to His purpose.

1. **Faith Beyond Feelings**: We do not move on by faith beyond our feelings. Some feelings are easier than others to have—feelings of being hurt, disappointed, and afraid come somewhat naturally. Certain, indeed most, of these feelings will be felt, but they should not determine or dictate what we do next. The very nature of faith requires acts of obedience to the Word of God, when by all appearances such actions contradict our feelings. It is acting in trust when one is not certain of the outcome.

2. **Faith is active, not passive**. Therefore, it becomes a matter not of passively waiting but of actively moving in the direction of the future coming from God for each of us. It means the taking of certain steps, as small as they may be, toward the future that God has ordained for us-perhaps to plunge back into ministry, perhaps the act of seeking reconciliation, or just a simple trust in God for what comes next. That's probably the reason why the Bible says, in James 2:17, "faith by itself, if it does not have works, is dead." Every day of our lives, each one of us acts and decides based on how much faith we have.

REBUILDING AFTER A SETBACK

There is a very important process of rebuilding after a conflict, failure, or burnout, and that is the rebuilding process. It calls for faith and wisdom with a sense of intentionality.

1. **Acknowledge the loss, the incident**: what has gone, or what has happened. Striving to pull through without mentioning the pain of the loss can actually end up blocking total healing and growth. It's okay to grieve the loss: be it a position, relationship, or a season in ministry. One can deal with it honestly before God only after he acknowledges the loss.

2. **Seek God's Wisdom**: Rebuilding takes wisdom, and wisdom comes from God. He beckons us to ask for wisdom in James 1:5, and He will give it liberally. Seeking God's leading through prayer, His Word, and the input of wise fellow believers is so vital in making known His will and the steps that He would have you take next. Ask God to reveal His will for you in this situation and lead you into His plans.

3. **Start Small and Be Patient**: Many times, rebuilding requires only starting in a small way and then being patient with the process. This may look like taking baby steps towards healing, re-engaging in ministry in small ways, or rebuilding trust with others just one small step at a time. Do not despise the day of small things (Zechariah 4:10): every obedient step in faith, moving forward, is one step toward recovery and growth.

4. **Set new boundaries**: Part of moving on is setting new and healthier boundaries that may have been breached in previous relationships.

Such boundaries could protect your heart, time, and energy. Whether it's being better at managing commitments or having clearer expectations in relationships, boundaries help a person not to commit the same mistake again.

5. **Surround Yourself with Support:** Overcoming a setback is not one of those things to do in isolation. Surround yourself with a support network of believers who encourage, pray, and walk with you in the process. The body of Christ is designed to help bear one another's burdens (Galatians 6:2).

LET GO OF THE PAST TO GRAB HOLD OF THE FUTURE

The hardest thing to ever let go of usually involves an attachment to the past. When we hold onto hurts, failures, or even successes from the past, it holds us back from fully embracing what God has for us in the future.

1. **Let go of bitterness and unforgiveness**. This is because it is very possible that bitterness and unforgiveness can make us captives of the past. At several places in the last chapter, we considered how important forgiveness is to healing and moving forward. Decide to let go before God of all the bitterness, resentment, and unforgiveness. This is not for the sake of the offender but for your setting free and growth.

2. **Forget What Lies Behind**: The Apostle Paul says in Philippians 3:13-14, "Forgetting what lies behind and straining forward to what lies ahead, I press on toward the goal for the prize of the upward call of God in Christ Jesus." Paul encourages us to forget the past—whether it be past glories or past failures—and press on toward the future that God has prepared for us. It does not mean forgetting and erasing memories but rather not dwelling on them.

3. **Reframe Your Perspective**: Look at the past, and instead of defeat or loss, see it as the perfect runner's block. Remember what God has taught you in and through the experience—the way it shapes your character, deepens your faith. With this reframed perspective, you get to look at your past in light of God's grace and purpose.

4. **Setting New Goals in Faith**: Moving on by faith requires setting new goals that are in line with the will of God. Pray for a new vision regarding the future. Establish goals that extend your faith and

require God's power to achieve. Whether it be a new ministry undertaking, personal growth, or deeper relationships, establish goals that will propel you forward.

GOD'S PROMISES FOR MOVING AHEAD IN FAITH

God's Word is replete with promises that provide us hope and confidence as we step out in faith. These assurances are anchors for the soul that works brilliantly against the tides of uncertainty and fear which affect us all at some time.

1. **God Is Always with You**: Probably the greatest assurance that we have as believers is the presence of God. In Joshua 1:9, God says, "Be strong and courageous. Do not be frightened, and do not be dismayed, for the Lord your God is with you wherever you go." Actually, whatever happens, we will have the confidence to stride forward into the unknown, for we know all along the way, God is with us.

2. **God Will Complete His Work in You**: As it says in Philippians 1:6, "He who began a good work in you will bring it to completion at the day of Jesus Christ." God is faithful to complete the work He has initiated in you. Sometimes things do not exactly go as planned, but even then God works, shapes, and is setting you up for His plan.

3. **God's Strength is Made Perfect in Weakness**: When we are feeling incapable of moving one more step forward, there is God's strength available. When we are weak, says God, in 2 Corinthians 12:9: "My grace is sufficient for you, for my power is made perfect in weakness." Often, moving on by faith will mean moving by the strength of God rather than our own.

4. **God's Agenda Is Full of Hope:** Jeremiah 29:11: "For I know the plans I have for you, declares the Lord, plans for welfare and not for evil, to give you a future and a hope." God has special plans for you, and these plans are good ones because he wants to give you a hope-filled future. So when your eyes can't see into a full picture, just know that His plans are falling into place for your good.

TALES OF OVERCOMING

Moving On by Faith Throughout the Bible, one can find many stories of individuals who suffered setbacks and turmoil and moved on by faith.

1. **Joseph's Story of Redemption**: Joseph's choice to move forward in faith, trusting God after his betrayal by his brothers, false accusation, and imprisonment, proved to be one of amazing redemption and restoration. What was intended for evil, God used for good-to bring about a greater purpose. Genesis 50:20 says that His ways are indeed higher than ours, as He can take our setbacks and turn them into setups for His glory.

2. **Ruth's Walk of Faith**: On the death of her husband, Ruth went ahead to continue life in faith and followed her widowed mother-in-law, Naomi, to a foreign country. Her faithfulness and willingness to go forward gave a place for her in the lineage of Jesus Christ. From the story of Ruth, we can tell that one can move forward in life by faith, having caused a drastic change in circumstances that had come as a shock to them.

3. **The Undaunted Ministry of Paul**: The apostle Paul suffered so much: he was persecuted, thrown into prison, and rejected. However, he kept living by faith as he continued to preach the Gospel and establish the Church. His life was such a powerful presentation of resilience and faith in the midst of adversity.

CONCLUSION (FAITH AS THE KEY TO MOVING ON)

Moving by faith is not always easy, but it is necessary if we are going to realize God's purpose in our lives. Trust is a deep heart commitment to God's sovereignty, a cold decision to move forward, and leaving all in the past. In faith lies the key to unlock new opportunities, fresh starts, and a deeper relationship with God. May you, as you choose to move on by faith, experience the freedom, joy, and fulfillment that comes from following God's lead.

CHAPTER 15

PRAYER VERSES ON FAITH

Prayer is an effective way of communicating with God, showing confidence in Him, and building the faith that has been instilled in one's heart. Indeed, there are several prayer verses found in the Bible that usher one into the ability to pray with faith, believe in what God has promised, and stand on the solidity of His Word. Below are some of the most important prayer Scriptures of faith. These will act as guidelines in your prayer life. These verses remind us of God's faithfulness, His promises, and a believing prayer's power. One way to align our hearts with His will and feel Him deeper in our relationship is through praying Scripture back to God.

PRAYING FOR INCREASED FAITH

The Bible encourages us to ask for faith to be increased. Faith is a gift of God, not something we can create in our hearts; and we may pray that God give us increase therein.

Mark 9:24: "Immediately the father of the child cried out and said, 'I believe; help my unbelief!'"

1. **Prayer Reflection:** Lord, I believe, just like the father in this story; yet at times, even I have to deal with doubt and unbelief. I ask You to help my unbelief and increase my faith. Give me strength to trust Your promises and to stand on Your Word when worldly circumstances would indicate the opposite. Strengthen my faith, Lord, so I might walk confidently in Your truth.

Luke 17:5 And the apostles said unto the Lord, Increase our faith.

2. **Prayer Reflection:** Father, I cry out with the disciples for You to increase my faith. Help me to believe and know that only You are my help in times of need and not my understanding or talents. I need to be grown in faith that moves mountains, faith that can be patient, faith that is pleasing to You. Show me the paths of righteousness, O Lord. Let me always trust in Your unfailing love.

PRAYING WITH BOLDNESS AND CONFIDENCE

The Scripture wants us to come boldly before God's throne of grace and is assured that He hears our prayers and answers them in accordance with His will.

Hebrews 4:16, "Let us then with confidence draw near to the throne of grace, that we may receive mercy and find grace to help in time of need."

1. **Prayer Reflection:** Lord, with confidence I come before Your throne of grace, knowing You are a loving and merciful God. Thank You for the privilege of prayer and the assurance that You hear me when I call. I ask for Your mercy and grace to help me in my time of need. Strengthen my heart to trust You more and to pray boldly, knowing You are faithful to answer.

1 John 5:14-15: "And this is the confidence that we have toward him, that if we ask anything according to his will he hears us. And if we know that he hears us in whatever we ask, we know that we have the requests that we have asked of him."

2. **Prayer Reflection**: Father in heaven, I pray in confidence, knowing You hear my prayers when I ask in accordance with Your will. Teach me to pray in concert with Your purpose and to trust in Your perfect timing. I believe You are a good Father who desires only to give good gifts to Your children. I pray, Your will be done in my life, trusting You for what is best.

PRAYING FOR FAITH TO OVERCOME FEAR AND ANXIETY

The antidote to fear is faith. The Word of God has equipped us with various scriptures that enable us to pray for faith to overcome anxiety, the worry bug, and fear.

Philippians 4:6-7: "Do not be anxious about anything, but in everything by prayer and supplication with thanksgiving let your requests be made known to God. And the peace of God, which surpasses all understanding, will guard your hearts and your minds in Christ Jesus."

1. **Prayer Reflection:** Lord, I lay down my anxieties and worries before You. I choose to trust You instead of giving into fear. Your Word says, "Do not be anxious about anything, but in everything, by prayer and petition, with thanksgiving, present your requests to God." I thank You for Your faithfulness and ask for Your peace that surpasses all understanding to guard my heart and mind in Christ Jesus. Enable me to rest in Your promises and have faith that You are in control.

Isaiah 41:10, "Fear not, for I am with you; be not dismayed, for I am your God; I will strengthen you, I will help you, I will uphold you with my righteous right hand."

2. **Prayer:** Father, I clung onto Your promise that I'm not to fear but You are with me. Give me strength in weakness, that I would lean upon Your presence and Your power. Uphold me with Your righteous right hand and give me courage to face every challenge in faith and not in fear. I put my trust in You, O God, my refuge and my strength.

PRAYING TO HAVE FAITH TO SEE THE IMPOSSIBLE BECOME POSSIBLE

Jesus taught that even the tiniest faith-a faith as small as that contained in a mustard seed-could move mountains. Sometimes we need faith to believe for the impossible, and the Lord invites us to ask for such faith.

Matthew 17:20 "He said to them, 'For truly, I say to you, if you have faith like a grain of mustard seed, you will say to this mountain, "Move from here to there," and it will move, and nothing will be impossible for you.'"

1. **Prayer Reflection:** Lord Jesus, You said that even if my faith be as small as a mustard seed, I can move mountains. I come to You, believing that with You nothing shall be impossible. Lord, give me faith to see beyond the natural and believe for the supernatural. Help me to trust in Your power to move the mountains in my life, standing

firmly on Your Word, knowing You are able to do exceedingly abundantly above all I ask or think.

Mark 11:24, "Whatever you ask in prayer, believe that you have received it and it will be yours."

2. **Prayer Reflection:** Father in heaven, I pray, believing I have received what I'm asking, as is Your will. Lord, help me learn to pray with an expectant heart, trusting Your promises, praying in faith and not doubting in my heart but believing You can do all I ask in Your name. I thank You for Your faithfulness, for I am assured that You hear and answer my prayer.

PRAYING FOR STEADFAST FAITH IN TRIALS AND SUFFERING

Trials and suffering have a way of coming our way, even when we least expect it. It is in these instances, however, that our faith can indeed be cultivated. Here are some Bible verses that instruct us on how to pray during such times for steadfast faith:.

James 1:2-4: "Count it all joy, my brothers, when you meet trials of various kinds, for you know that the testing of your faith produces steadfastness. And let steadfastness have its full effect, that you may be perfect and complete, lacking in nothing.".

1. **Prayer Reflection**: Lord, help me to count it all joy when I face trials and difficulties. I know the testing of my faith produces steadiness; hence, I ask You to help me stand steady in the midst of my challenges. Let these trials shape me and make me more like You. I trust that You are using every circumstance to build my character and to bring me to maturity in Christ.

1 Peter 5:10 After you have suffered for a little while, God himself, the God of all grace, who called you to his eternal glory in Christ, after you have suffered a little while, will himself restore, confirm, strengthen and establish you.

2. **Prayer Reflection:** God of all grace, I thank You that after I have suffered for a little while, You will restore, confirm, strengthen, and establish me. I know Your faithfulness will see me through, as Your promises declare. Lord, may my faith be strengthened to endure and emerge from these trials even stronger, rooted deeper into You.

PRAYING FOR FAITH TO WALK IN GOD'S PROMISES

The Bible is filled with promises given by God to His children. The action of praying those promises back to God is one way we turn the "on" switch of our faith and willfully align our will and desires with His.

2 Corinthians 1:20 For all the promises of God find their Yes in him. That is why it is through him that we utter our Amen to God for his glory.

1. **Prayer Reflection:** Lord, I thank You that all Your promises find their Yes in Christ. I claim Your promises over my life and ask for the faith to walk in them. Help me to trust in Your Word, and to believe what You have promised You are faithful to fulfill. May my life be a testimony of Your faithfulness and glory.

Hebrews 11:1: "Now faith is the assurance of things hoped for, the conviction of things not seen.".

2. **Prayer Reflection:** Father, I pray that my faith would be assurance of things hoped for, conviction of things not seen. Sometimes, help me to believe in those things which I'm promised, but oftentimes am not able to discern with my natural eyes. May my hope be anchored in You, and may my faith continue growing stronger as I trust Your unfailing love and faithfulness.

CONCLUSION (PRAYER LIFE BUILT ON THE FOUNDATION OF FAITH)

Praying Scripture is one of the most potent ways to build our faith and draw closer in relationship with God. These prayer verses about faith lead us in confidently, boldly, and

1. **Expectation:** As we pray God's Word back to Him, our hearts are aligned with His will, and we grow in trust of His promises. May we be encouraged to pray in faith, knowing that He hears and is faithful to answer.

CHAPTER 16

PRAYER VERSES ON FORGIVENESS

Forgiveness is at the very core of our being as Christian people: a profound action about love, humility, and obedience to the Word of God. In seeking to forgive others or to know the forgiveness of God, we find helpful shaping of prayers in Scripture. The Bible is filled with verses that speak to the power and necessity of forgiveness both in our relationship with God and our relationships with others. This chapter gives prayer verses on forgiveness that will help us reflect upon, repent, and release bitterness or any unforgiveness we have held unto.

PRAYING FOR GOD'S FORGIVENESS AND CLEANSING

Excerpts from the Bible show that all have sinned and fallen short of the glory of God, but God is gracious, and He wants to forgive those who come to Him with a repentant heart.

1 John 1:9: "If we confess our sins, he is faithful and just to forgive us our sins and to cleanse us from all unrighteousness."

1. **Prayer Reflection:** Lord, I come before You, confessing my sins, and acknowledging that I have fallen short of Your glory. Thank You for Your promise that if I confess my sins, You are faithful and just to forgive me and cleanse me from all unrighteousness. I ask for Your forgiveness; I ask that You give me a clean heart. Wash me with Your precious blood and make me new. Help me walk in your righteousness, and also grant that my life will be pleasing to you.

Psalm 51:10: "Create in me a clean heart, O God, and renew a right spirit within me."

2. **Prayer Reflection:** Dear Abba Father, I pray just as David did, saying, "Create in me a clean heart, O God. Renew a right spirit within me." Take away the stain of my sin and help me to walk clean and holy. Allow my life to speak volumes to others of Your love, Your grace, and Your forgiveness. Teach me to seek out Your face at every turn, and teach me to lean upon Your strength when temptation rears its ugly head.

PRAYING TO FORGIVE OTHERS AS GOD FORGIVES US

We know very well that forgiving others is not easy, but God commands us to do this. Since God forgives us, we need to forgive others.

Matthew 6:14-15: "For if you forgive others their trespasses, your heavenly Father will also forgive you, but if you do not forgive others their trespasses, neither will your Father forgive your trespasses."

1. **Prayer Reflection:** Lord, I understand the importance of forgiving others as You have forgiven me. Help me obtain the graces to rid my heart of all unforgiveness. Help me to forgive those who hurt or wronged me because I, too, am in need of Your mercy and forgiveness. Give me the strength to let go of bitterness, resentment, and anger. Teach me to walk in love and to extend the same grace to others that You have shown to me.

Colossians 3:13, "Bearing with one another and, if one has a complaint against another, forgiving each other; as the Lord has forgiven you, so you also must forgive."

2. **Prayer Reflection:** Father, help me to bear with others in love and to forgive those that have hurt me. I know I am called to forgive as You have forgiven me. Help me learn to be quick to forgive and slow to anger. I cast every offense to You and ask for Your healing touch upon my heart. Fill me with Your peace and love so I can be the reflection of Your grace towards others.

PRAYER FOR A HEART OF COMPASSION AND MERCY

God wants us to have a heart full of compassion and mercy, just as He does. In asking to pray for a forgiving heart, one is asking God to grant him the capability to be compassionate and understanding.

Ephesians 4:32: "Be kind to one another, tenderhearted, forgiving one another, as God in Christ forgave you."

1. **Prayer Reflection:** Lord, I pray that You give me a tender heart, quick to forgive and slow to hold grudges. Help me to show others kindness and compassion when it doesn't come easily. Let Your love fill my heart, that I may extend forgiveness and grace as You have forgiven me in Christ. Help me to be a vessel of Your love and mercy.

Micah 7:18 Who is a God like you, who pardons iniquity, and passes over the transgression of the remnant of his heritage? He does not retain his anger for ever because he delights in steadfast love.

2. **Prayer Reflection:** Father in heaven, I praise Your name, because You are a God who forgives iniquity and loves covenant loyalty. Help me to be like You-offering forgiveness, and not holding any grudges or bitterness. Anoint me to learn Your ways of forgiveness, to love others just like You have loved me. Let my heart be in constant harmony with Yours.

PRAYING FOR THE GRACE TO OVERCOME HURT AND OFFENSE

Forgiveness often involves having to overcome deep hurt and offense. Forgive by releasing the pain through God's grace.

Proverbs 19:11: "Good sense makes one slow to anger, and it is his glory to overlook an offense.".

1. **Prayer for Reflection:** Dear Lord, I ask You for the wisdom and good sense to be slow to anger and overlook offenses. Help me in rising above hurt feelings with graciousness and insight. I know that harbouring offence harms me. Teach me to let go my offence and

simply trust in Your justice and timing. My heart, I pray, will be filled with Your peace and love.

Matthew 18:21-22: "Then came Peter to him, and said, Lord, how oft shall my brother sin against me, and I forgive him? till seven times? Jesus saith unto him, I say not unto thee, Until seven times: but, Until seventy times seven."

2. **Prayer Reflection:** Lord Jesus, You taught us to forgive not just seven times but seventy times seven. Help me to be always prepared in my heart to forgive no matter how many times I am wronged. Give me the ability not to hold grudges but to forgive without counting. I know it, and I am aware that forgiveness is not an act; it is a continuous choice to walk in love and grace. Give me strength to forgive like You have forgiven me.

PRAYING FOR RECONCILIATION AND RESTORATION

Forgiveness is often accompanied by reconciliation and the re-establishing of lost relationships. We can pray for God to heal where there has been division and restore unity.

2 Corinthians 5:18-19: "All this is from God, who through Christ reconciled us to himself and gave us the ministry of reconciliation; that is, in Christ God was reconciling the world to himself, not counting their trespasses against them, and entrusting to us the message of reconciliation."

1. **Prayer Reflection:** Father, thank You for reconciling me to Yourself through Christ. I pray for reconciliation and restoration in my relationships where there has been hurt or division. Enable me to be Your agent of peace, and to carry on the ministry of reconciliation. Let me be swift to forgive, seeking restoration in living in harmony with others. May Your love bring healing and unity.

Romans 12:18 "If possible, so far as it depends on you, live peaceably with all.".

2. **Prayer Reflection:** Lord, I would like to live in peace with all people as far as it is possible on my part. Reveal to me where I need to seek forgiveness and where I need to extend it. Help me to pursue

peace and reconciliation in all my relationships. Give me the courage to take the first step in repairing fractured relationships and to be a peacemaker in my home, community, and beyond.

PRAYER FOR FORGIVENESS TO FEEL FREE

Forgiveness is not just about setting people free, but it also pertains to an experience of freedom. Unforgiveness chains us in chains, and forgiving sets us free.

Galatians 5:1, "For freedom, Christ has set us free; stand firm, therefore, and do not submit again to a yoke of slavery.

1. **Prayer Reflection:** Lord, thank You for the freedom that I have in Christ. Help me to stand in that freedom and not become enslaved to bitterness or unforgiveness. I choose to release those who have hurt me and walk in the liberty You have given to me. May my heart be free from any weight of unforgiveness so that I may serve You fully in Your grace and love.

Matthew 5:23-24: "So if you are offering your gift at the altar and there remember that your brother has something against you, leave your gift there before the altar and go. First be reconciled to your brother, and then come and offer your gift.".

2. **Prayer Reflection:** Lord, I do not want anything to come between You and me. If there is anyone I need to forgive or seek forgiveness from, show me. Help me to take immediate action to be reconciled. I want my worship and prayers to be pleasing to You. Give me the courage and humility to make things right and to live in harmony with others.

CONCLUSION (A LIFE WRAPPED IN FORGIVENESS)

Forgiveness may not always be easy, but it's a given mandate for our spiritual development and health. While we pray these Scriptures, let's ask God to help us forgive as He forgives us, love others as He loves us, and extend grace as He extends it to us. May we embrace the pattern of a life wrapped in forgiveness-the very reflection of the heart of our Heavenly Father-so that we also may be set free when you forgive your pure heart.

CHAPTER 17

PRAYER VERSES ON TRUSTING IN GOD

Trusting in God is a foundational aspect of the Christian faith. It involves surrendering our will and placing our confidence in God's wisdom, power, and love, even when circumstances are challenging. The Bible is filled with verses that encourage us to trust in God, to lean not on our own understanding, and to find peace in His presence. This chapter provides prayer verses that help us build our trust in God through prayer and reflection.

TRUSTING GOD'S PLANS AND PURPOSES

God has a purpose and plan for each of our lives. Trusting in His plans means believing that He knows what is best for us and that His ways are higher than ours.

- **Jeremiah 29:11**: "For I know the plans I have for you, declares the Lord, plans for welfare and not for evil, to give you a future and a hope."

1. **Prayer Reflection*:*** Heavenly Father, I thank You that You have plans for my life—plans for my welfare, to give me a future and a hope. Even when I do not see the full picture, help me to trust in Your plans. Guide me to walk in the path that You have set for me. Give me patience to wait on You and the faith to believe that You are working all things together for my good.

- **Proverbs 3:5-6**: "Trust in the Lord with all your heart, and do not lean on your own understanding. In all your ways acknowledge him, and he will make straight your paths."

2. **Prayer Reflection***:* Lord, I choose to trust You with all my heart and not to lean on my own understanding. I surrender my thoughts, my plans, and my fears to You. In all my ways, I acknowledge You. Lead me and guide me on the path You have prepared for me. Make my path straight and help me to walk in alignment with Your will.

TRUSTING GOD IN TIMES OF TROUBLE AND UNCERTAINTY

Life can be full of uncertainties and trials, but God invites us to trust Him even in the most difficult moments. His presence is a constant source of comfort and strength.

- **Psalm 46:1**: "God is our refuge and strength, a very present help in trouble."

1. **Prayer Reflection***:* Lord, You are my refuge and strength, a very present help in times of trouble. I turn to You in my distress and place my trust in Your mighty power. I know that You are with me and that You will never leave me nor forsake me. Surround me with Your peace that surpasses all understanding and help me to rest in the assurance of Your protection.

- **Isaiah 41:10**: "Fear not, for I am with you; be not dismayed, for I am your God; I will strengthen you, I will help you, I will uphold you with my righteous right hand."

2. **Prayer Reflection***:* Father, I choose not to fear, for I know You are with me. I will not be dismayed, for You are my God. Strengthen me in my weakness and help me to stand firm in faith. Uphold me with Your righteous right hand and guide me through every storm. I trust that You are my protector and that You are working for my good.

TRUSTING GOD'S PROVISION AND CARE

God promises to provide for our needs and to care for us as His children. Trusting Him means believing that He is our ultimate provider and sustainer.

- **Philippians 4:19**: "And my God will supply every need of yours according to his riches in glory in Christ Jesus."

1. **Prayer Reflection*:*** Lord, I thank You for Your promise to supply all my needs according to Your riches in glory in Christ Jesus. I trust in Your provision and care. Help me to rely on You and not to worry about tomorrow. Teach me to live in contentment, knowing that You are my provider and that You care for me deeply.

- **Matthew 6:31-33**: "Therefore do not be anxious, saying, 'What shall we eat?' or 'What shall we drink?' or 'What shall we wear?'... But seek first the kingdom of God and his righteousness, and all these things will be added to you."

2. ***Prayer Reflection*:** Father, I seek first Your kingdom and Your righteousness, trusting that all other things will be added unto me. Help me not to be anxious about my daily needs but to rest in Your faithful provision. You know what I need even before I ask. I trust You to provide and guide me each step of the way.

TRUSTING GOD'S TIMING

God's timing is perfect, even when it doesn't align with our own desires. Trusting His timing means being patient and waiting on Him to act in His own way and time.

- **Ecclesiastes 3:11**: "He has made everything beautiful in its time. Also, he has put eternity into man's heart, yet so that he cannot find out what God has done from the beginning to the end."

1. **Prayer Reflection*:*** Lord, I know that You make everything beautiful in its time. Teach me to trust in Your perfect timing and to be patient in the waiting. Help me to surrender my own timeline to You and to trust that You are working all things for good. Give me peace in the process and the faith to know that Your ways are higher than mine.

- **Psalm 27:14**: "Wait for the Lord; be strong, and let your heart take courage; wait for the Lord!"

2. **Prayer Reflection*:*** Father, I choose to wait on You and to be strong in faith. Give me courage to trust You even when the wait seems long. Strengthen my heart to hold onto Your promises and to believe

that You are faithful to fulfill them. Help me to be still and know that You are God, working in ways I cannot see.

TRUSTING GOD'S PROMISES

God's promises are true and trustworthy. Trusting in His promises means believing that what He has said will come to pass.

- **Numbers 23:19**: "God is not man, that he should lie, or a son of man, that he should change his mind. Has he said, and will he not do it? Or has he spoken, and will he not fulfill it?"

1. **Prayer Reflection*:*** Lord, I trust in Your promises because I know You are not a man that You should lie. What You have spoken, You will fulfill. Help me to stand firm on Your Word and to believe in Your faithfulness. Even when doubt tries to creep in, let me hold fast to Your truth and be reminded that You are always true to Your Word.

- **Psalm 145:13**: "The Lord is faithful in all his words and kind in all his works."

2. **Prayer Reflection*:*** Father, I thank You for Your faithfulness in all Your words and for Your kindness in all Your works. I trust that every promise You have made will come to pass. Help me to remember Your faithfulness in times of waiting and uncertainty. Let Your Word be a lamp to my feet and a light to my path, guiding me in truth.

TRUSTING GOD COMPLETELY IN EVERY AREA OF LIFE

Trusting God involves every area of our lives—our relationships, decisions, finances, health, and future. We are invited to cast all our cares upon Him, knowing He cares for us.

- **Psalm 37:5**: "Commit your way to the Lord; trust in him, and he will act."

1. **Prayer Reflection*:*** Lord, I commit my way to You and trust in You completely. I know that You will act on my behalf according to Your perfect will. Help me not to take matters into my own hands but to

surrender every area of my life to You. I trust that You will lead me and guide me in the way I should go.

- **1 Peter 5:7**: "Casting all your anxieties on him, because he cares for you."

2. **Prayer Reflection***:* Father, I cast all my anxieties and cares upon You, for I know You care for me. Help me to let go of fear, worry, and control. Teach me to trust You with every aspect of my life. May I rest in Your love and find peace in Your presence, knowing that You are holding me in the palm of Your hand.

CONCLUSION (LIVING A LIFE OF TRUST IN GOD)

Trusting in God is a daily journey of surrender and faith. As we pray these Scriptures and meditate on God's Word, we are reminded of His unfailing love, faithfulness, and power. Let us choose to trust God completely, knowing that He is always working for our good and His glory. May our hearts be filled with peace as we place our trust in Him who holds all things together.

CHAPTER 18
WOE TO THE SHEPHERDS WHO DESTROY AND SCATTER THE SHEEP

Jeremiah 23:1-6 (NKJV) states:

"Woe to the shepherds who destroy and scatter the sheep of My pasture!" says the LORD. Therefore thus says the LORD God of Israel against the shepherds who feed My people: "You have scattered My flock, driven them away, and not attended to them."

This passage is a stern warning to spiritual leaders—often referred to as shepherds—who, through negligence, abuse, or poor leadership, cause harm to God's people. The "sheep" in this metaphor represent the congregation, while the shepherds symbolize pastors, priests, or leaders who are responsible for guiding, nurturing, and protecting their flock. However, when these leaders fail in their duties, the consequences are devastating.

THE RESPONSIBILITIES OF A SHEPHERD

The role of a shepherd is critical in the life of the church. They are tasked with feeding, protecting, guiding, and nurturing the flock entrusted to them by God. The responsibilities include:

1. Providing Spiritual Nourishment: Shepherds must deliver God's Word faithfully, teaching sound doctrine that edifies and grows the congregation spiritually.
2. Protecting from Harm: Shepherds should guard the flock from false teachings, divisive behaviors, and any spiritual or moral dangers.
3. Guiding with Wisdom and Love: Shepherds are to lead by example, modeling Christlike behavior and guiding the flock with love, patience, and humility.

4. Caring for the Weak and Wounded: They must be attentive to those who are hurting, offering pastoral care and support.

However, when these duties are neglected or when shepherds abuse their positions, the sheep are left vulnerable, hurt, and scattered.

HOW SHEPHERDS DESTROY AND SCATTER

A pastor or leader can unintentionally (or at times, intentionally) cause offense or division within a church through various actions or behaviors. Here are some common ways that shepherds may fail in their duties:

1. Showing Favoritism: When a pastor consistently gives special attention or preference to certain members or groups, it can lead to feelings of exclusion, jealousy, and resentment among others. This can create divisions and cliques within the church.
2. Harsh or Insensitive Preaching: Using the pulpit to shame, condemn, or attack individuals or groups rather than building up the congregation with truth and love can alienate members and cause them to leave the church.
3. Gossip and Slander: Speaking negatively about others behind their backs, even under the guise of "prayer concerns" or counsel, damages trust and creates a toxic environment within the church community.
4. Ignoring or Mishandling Conflicts: Failing to address conflicts or handling them poorly can lead to festering issues, divisions, and broken relationships within the church, causing members to scatter.
5. Abusing Authority: When a pastor uses their position to manipulate, control, or intimidate others, it fosters a culture of fear and distrust, leading many to be hurt or leave the church.
6. Neglecting Pastoral Care: Failing to care for or minister to those in need—whether due to busyness, indifference, or a focus on other priorities—can cause members to feel neglected and unimportant.
7. Inconsistent or Hypocritical Behavior: When a pastor's private life contradicts their public teaching, it causes disillusionment and spiritual harm, leading to offense, mistrust, and members leaving the church.

THE DANGERS OF LEADING WHILE BLEEDING

A particular challenge that shepherds face is leading while dealing with their own unresolved pain, trauma, or spiritual wounds—a concept often referred to as "leading while bleeding." This can have several significant negative effects:

1. Projecting Hurt onto Others: Leaders who are hurting may inadvertently project their pain, bitterness, or unresolved issues onto the congregation, leading to harsh treatment, unfair judgment, or misplaced anger.
2. Burnout and Fatigue: Carrying personal burdens while trying to care for others often leads to emotional, spiritual, and physical exhaustion. This can result in burnout, where a leader becomes ineffective or steps down.
3. Poor Decision-Making: Pain and unresolved issues can cloud judgment and hinder a leader's ability to make sound, Spirit-led decisions. Choices made from a place of hurt often lack wisdom and can negatively impact the church or organization.
4. Erosion of Trust: If congregants sense that a leader is leading from a place of hurt, they may lose confidence in that leader's ability to guide them spiritually. Trust is critical in pastoral relationships, and leading while bleeding can erode that trust.

WHEN TRUST IS BROKEN

Trust is foundational in any church community. When a pastor does not trust the staff and members of the church, or when members no longer trust their shepherd, the consequences are severe:

1. Micromanagement and Control: A lack of trust often leads to micromanagement, where the pastor feels the need to oversee every detail and decision, creating an environment where staff and members feel stifled and undervalued.
2. Poor Team Morale: When staff and members sense they are not trusted, it can lead to low morale, resentment, and disengagement. This causes them to lose motivation and passion for ministry.
3. Communication Breakdowns: A lack of trust often leads to poor or guarded all communications, and resulting in confusion,

misunderstandings, and a lack of collaboration within the church.

4. High Turnover and Burnout: When staff and volunteers feel mistrusted, they are more likely to experience burnout or seek opportunities elsewhere. High turnover can lead to instability within the church and difficulty maintaining continuity in ministry efforts.

THE IMPORTANCE OF HEALING AND RECONCILIATION

When church members experience hurt and rejection, it can deeply wound their spiritual, emotional, and social well-being. The struggles they face can range from a loss of trust in leadership to spiritual disillusionment, isolation, bitterness, difficulty engaging in worship and ministry, fear of vulnerability, and more. Overcoming church hurt and rejection requires intentional healing, often through counseling, forgiveness, and finding a supportive and loving church community. Acknowledging the hurt, seeking God's comfort, and slowly rebuilding trust are vital steps toward restoration and spiritual renewal.

CONCLUSION (A CALL TO FAITHFUL SHEPHERDING)

Jeremiah's prophecy is a sobering reminder that God holds shepherds accountable for the well-being of His flock. Spiritual leaders are called to lead with integrity, humility, and love, always seeking to build up rather than tear down. They must be vigilant in guarding against behaviors that scatter and destroy, choosing instead to nurture and care for God's people faithfully.

God promises to raise up shepherds after His own heart, who will lead with wisdom, love, and righteousness. May all who are called to shepherd His people heed this warning, seek healing where needed, and strive to build healthy, Christ-centered communities where His flock can thrive and grow. To instruct Leaders to remember to **Love one another** and Your Enemy and the scripture saying Remember to **Return to your First Love**. Also remember Jesus said,

"FEED MY SHEEP"

Shepherds, will **You** not leave the ninety-nine on the mountains and go insearch of the one that went astray!

Made in the USA
Columbia, SC
23 March 2025